MW01265609

A Hard Day's Devotional

DAILY BLESSINGS FOR BRUISED BOOMERS

Brad Wiewel

TRILOGY CHRISTIAN PUBLISHERS
TUSTIN, CA

Trilogy Christian Publishers
A Wholly Owned Subsidiary of Trinity Broadcasting Network
2442 Michelle Drive
Tustin, CA 92780

Manufactured in the United States of America

10 9 8 7 6 5 4 3 2 1

Library of Congress Cataloging-in-Publication Data is available.

ISBN: 978-1-63769-090-1

E-ISBN: 978-1-63769-091-8 (ebook)

Introduction

Why *A Hard Day's Devotional?* Well, I have been a daily Bible reader for over thirty years. Since I began this practice (which I highly recommend), I was struck by the number of times the words "bless," "blesses," "blessed," and "blessing" were used. I couldn't see a specific pattern, but when I did some research, I discovered those words, or a combination of them, occur more than any other term God uses other than "love," "holy," "evil," and "sin."

My conclusion is *He must have had a purpose for that.*

What is set out in the next 365 pages may explain this purpose. There are many different uses of those words by everyone, from God in Genesis 1:22 all the way to John in Revelation 22:14. Sometimes the words are meant to be just that—a blessing. At other times, however, turmoil and pain are present.

Aren't our lives as baby boomers like that, too? We may feel bruised by all the cultural changes afflicting our society and experience frustration, disappointment, and, yes, blessings. As you study these pages each day, I believe you will find the three primary keys to being blessed: Faith, Love, and Obedience.

I pray you enjoy this book, and hopefully, the thoughts recorded here will help us all see God's blessings more often, thank Him for them, and use those words to act, think, and speak more like Him.

To quote Tiny Tim, "God bless us, everyone!"

Powerhouse

God *blessed* them and said, "Be fruitful and increase in number and fill the waters in the seas, and let the birds increase on the earth."

Genesis 1:22

(hereafter, emphasis added)

Blessed. What a powerful word! Someone greater than us has decided to be more than kind, more than generous. A blessing is completely unmerited and bestowed because of love and affection. It is never from our efforts.

To put it frankly, God's love for us makes little sense. We are always messing up, we rarely ask for forgiveness, and we usually acknowledge Him only when we have reached rock bottom. Still, He loves us because He created us, just the way parents love a child who often ignores them.

But as we mature in faith, is striving to be more like Him the best we can do?

Let's resolve to spend this year focused more on our Heavenly Father, and less on ourselves. Although we'll never deserve His blessings, hopefully, we'll be better at recognizing them and showing Him gratitude for all of them.

Focus on being a powerhouse of prayer and action this year, starting today.

Bring It On

O Lord Almighty, *blessed* is the one who trusts
in you.

Psalm 84:12

Each new year can bring a combination of optimism
and fright. We're hopeful about what the future holds,
but in the back of our minds, we're anxious it may be
the opposite of the good we've imagined.

The truth is we can only trust God.

We are powerless to change any of it in our own
strength, as much as we like to believe that we can.

Yet trust is not a blind belief; it is an active knowledge that regardless of how things look or feel, Someone who loves us has put us here, and He will not leave
us alone.

Facing a future with an Almighty Father makes us
powerful.

Trust is what fills us with an attitude of invincibility,
not inevitability.

Say "Bring it on, Lord!" out loud today.

Pure and Simple

There, in the presence of the Lord your God, you and your families will eat and shall rejoice in everything you have put your hand to, because the Lord your God has *blessed you*.

Deuteronomy 12:7

"If someone wants to be nice to you, let them." That's a nice proverb, but it's much easier said than done. Safe to say we all want total control, even if someone is just trying to be nice. We are addicted to control, and if we accept help, we often do it grudgingly. We repeatedly think we aren't worthy of His blessings because of our constant screw-ups.

Because of this, we need to rethink our attitude toward God. Since we don't know what will happen this year, or even in the next ten minutes, asking Him to bless us right now is really an acknowledgement that He actually has the power to act, and that He loves us, warts and all.

Remember that a blessing we receive from Him today isn't based on our behavior; it's based on His love, pure and simple.

Pain Management

Blessed are all who take refuge in Him.
Psalm 2:12b

Nobody in their right mind likes physical pain, but we will run from emotional or mental pain even faster. Yet, pain cannot be escaped. It is all around us: it invades our days, and it knows where we live.

Like it or not, this side of Heaven, we are never done with pain.

When we see a close friend or family member experiencing pain, we often feel helpless or inadequate. We are often unable to offer more than a sympathetic shrug or hug.

This is exactly why Jesus is here.

He knows pain excruciatingly well—every kind of pain. And He has conquered it for us. Because He has been through every type of pain we could possibly endure, Jesus is now our refuge, our cave, our bomb shelter. We can run to Him as our sanctuary to escape the enemy who is constantly attacking us, the enemy who is hurting our friends, our family, or, most often, ourselves.

Jesus wants to take your pain. He gladly accepts it. He will be our refuge. Our hiding place from the storm of pain.

Ask for His help today...and be ready to accept it.

A Friend in Need

Blessed are those who listen to me, watching
daily at my doors, waiting at my doorway.
Proverbs 8:34

True friends are few and far between. Sometimes
our families, co-workers, and even pets fill in the
blanks. Genuine, intimate friends—when they exist—
help shoulder our burdens. They listen patiently and
allow us to talk as long as we need. Not many people
volunteer for that job.

So how about God?

Well, that's exactly what prayer is about. It is com-
plaining, crying, laughing or just talking to Him. Prayer
is God listening to us whine or whisper about our day,
our week, our month and our life. And He lets us do so
for as long as necessary. It is His job, and He loves to
do it.

When you have an intimate conversation with your
Heavenly Father, talk as long as you need, yell, scream
and even demand, based on promises in His Word.
He understands, and He appreciates honest, open
communication.

What we receive from Him is His calming presence,
wisdom, and assurance.

The Gospels show us that Jesus was the friend of tax
collectors and sinners. He'll be our friend today, too; we
just have to ask Him!

Misplaced Priorities

The man who was dying *blessed* me; I made the widow's heart sing.

Job 29:13

After a severe drought, a news report warned the new danger was flooding; the rain finally returned. How often do we complain about the heat, then the cold, or the drought and then the rain? What keeps us from giving thanks for what we have regardless of whether the weather is good or bad?

The answer is *pride*. We always want things "just so."

The truth is, we are insecure in our faith, so we want to control *everything*, and when we can't, we complain. We first complain to ourselves, then to anyone who will listen, and finally, we complain to God because this is ultimately *His fault*!

No, it is not.

The man who was dying *blessed* Job because he understood that when we die, our constant worries in life are no longer important. We will always have something to worry about if we so choose, yet our priority at death won't be money, status or looks.

What are your real priorities for today?

Prime Time

Oh, for the days when I was in my prime, when God's intimate friendship *blessed* my house.

Job 29:4

When does our prime time end? We all hope not too soon. We convince ourselves in hindsight that our prime is when we were in total control of our lives.

Yet, that is not true.

The truth is we don't really hit our prime until we realize we cannot control anything. God is in control. Always!

Job suffered and doubted. So do we. Our prime time ends when we feel we have no further future—when we have a sense of hopelessness. This is where Job was when he uttered this verse. When we finish Job's story, however, it becomes clear that what he thought was the end of the game was only halftime.

Let's remember that with Jesus we always have a future. With Him, our prime time is now, so let's start acting like it.

Your prime time starts today.

Ouch!

Blessed is the one you discipline, Lord; the one you teach from your law.

Psalm 94:12

The sentiment expressed in this Psalm sounds warm and encouraging, doesn't it? But who really wants to be disciplined?

None of us.

As we all know, we'll do a lot to avoid any sort of pain, let alone the kind inflicted by the Almighty. Still, when He catches up to us, and discipline is administered, we always know He is right, and we're wrong yet again.

At least we should.

Ultimately, we should be glad He didn't give us what we deserve, a knock-out punch.

When God finally gets our attention, which is never easy, we grasp His righteousness and usually accept our failures and inadequacies, at least temporarily. We repent and remorsefully promise we'll do better going forward.

Then we promptly forget.

Instead, we should be grateful He lay the full weight of our sins upon Jesus. When He does discipline us, we should be grateful for His mercy.

Pray for His mercy today.

Grow Baby Grow

Then God *blessed* Noah and his sons, saying to them, "Be fruitful and increase in number and fill the earth."

Genesis 9:1

Weekend-radio garden shows are popular because they ignore the rest of the world and focus on the basics. For example, a common question might be: "How do I grow better tomatoes?" There is no talk about politics, terrorism, family issues, or religion. Growing plants don't care who the President is, or what kept us awake last night. Plants have specific, basic needs in order to grow well.

While we often want God to be more involved in the world and our particular problems, He really has more of a focused, garden-show approach. He has provided all we need to thrive, so He wants us to tune out the distractions and grow into the person He wants us to be.

God's approach is more about each of us individually and less about everything else. Our Heavenly Father wants us to reach our full potential in Him, just like a master gardener wants his asparagus to be perfect.

To grow in Jesus today, tune out the excess, and focus on the basics.

Give and Get

The generous will themselves be *blessed*, for
they will share their food with the poor.

Proverbs 22:9

We all like to get free things. Whether it's saving
money with a coupon, or getting air miles with the
right credit card, free is always good!

God is definitely in the business of giving things
away. Salvation, for instance, is totally free. When you
understand what this cost God, it should blow your
mind, but even though it is free, we still have to accept
His offer of grace through faith.

From what Solomon tells us in this verse, when we
follow God's example, He will reward us for sharing
with those less fortunate. When we give things away
free, we are *blessed* by Him in return (and often, it comes
with a tax deduction! Not a bad deal, right?)

God has made giving as attractive as possible, so
what's your plan for this year? Remember the spiritual
law: the more we give, the more we are given.[1]

Give to Him and to others, and get a blessing today.

Core Values

See, I am setting before you today a *blessing*
and a curse.
Deuteronomy 11:26

Company "retreats" are meetings where employees
contemplate the future direction of the organization.
Outside speakers are often brought in to inspire and
shake things up, which leads to a discussion on the
company's core values.

Realigning the team with the firm's core values not
only reminds everyone of the definition of the firm's
purpose but is also meant to inspire everyone to perform at a higher level.

In the same way, it is healthy to periodically ask ourselves, "What are my core values?" An abundant bank
account? A happy family? A successful retirement fund?
These may be virtuous goals, but far more important is
the question we should all be asking ourselves: "What
are God's core values for us?"

Did you know the prophet Micah answered these
questions for us? He said God's core values for us are to
do justice, to love mercy, and to walk humbly before our God.[2]

Knowing the answer is only half the solution, however. We still need to align our core values with His.
How do we do this? By prayer, reading scripture, and
church attendance.

God has set before us a *blessing* and a curse. He has
provided His core values for us to follow. Whose are
more likely to bring *blessing* today? His or ours?

Nice to Be Noticed

Her mother-in-law asked her, "Where did you glean today? Where did you work? *Blessed* be the man who took notice of you!"

Ruth 2:19

It is nice to be noticed, isn't it? It's rare, however, that we're noticed for anything good. Usually, only our screw-ups are seen...things like a burnt meal, or a poor choice of words.

What is so good about God is that He notices us all the time.

Sure, we often wished He didn't. He notices our victories and our sins. He notices when we take the credit, and when we rightly defer it to Him. He notices when we love our neighbors, and when we are selfish.

Although He notices all the garbage in our lives, the astounding thing is He still loves us. He is still good to us, and we can still approach Him, asking for help with even the most trivial things. What a Guy!

Be assured that God notices you and loves you—He is always here today.

Blown Opportunity

An inheritance claimed too soon will not be
blessed in the end.

Proverbs 20:21

We assume *blessings* are always good things, right?
We got the job; we recovered from sickness; we received an inheritance...how could a *blessing* be bad? It
seems almost impossible, but it happens. How?

A *blessing* can turn bad because of the selfishness of
human nature.

A spouse is a *blessing* until we start to take them for
granted; a job is a *blessing* until we don't get a raise; children are *blessings* until they disappoint us; an inheritance is a *blessing* until we're tempted to squander it.

The reason inheritances are often blown overnight
is the recipient didn't acknowledge the work that went
into creating the wealth. Not appreciating the immense
effort that it takes to create an estate is what leads to the
problem Solomon describes in this scripture. The bottom line is we deserve nothing, yet we receive so much.

The solution is to focus on the one true inheritance
that supersedes all others.

Christ's promise of salvation—despite our sin-
fulness—is the only inheritance we should strive to
receive.

Don't blow the opportunities He's provided today.

Common Sense

Blessed is the man who does not walk in the counsel of the wicked or stand in the way of sinners or sit in the seat of mockers.

Psalm 1:1

Remember high school? When we all wanted to be like the popular kids who were cool and could get away with anything? Remember, too, when peer pressure was everywhere, and we couldn't escape it?

Now, as allegedly mature adults, we tend to believe we're immune to peer pressure. The truth is we're not. The social, personal and business lives of our friends and coworkers carry tremendous influence if left unchecked. The lives of those close to us can seem carefree and exciting, and if we're not careful, it can be nearly impossible to escape their influence, whether that influence is good or bad.

God gives us a very clear warning here. The common phrase, "Bad company corrupts good morals," echoes the truth of this scripture: surrounding ourselves with ungodly, worldly people leads to ungodly, worldly behavior. Surrounding ourselves with godly, upright people will help us lead godly, upright lives.

This knowledge isn't rocket science; it's common sense. So let's get busy and apply it today.

Much Too Much

Since the people began to bring their contributions to the temple of the Lord, we have had enough to eat and plenty to spare, because the Lord has *blessed* His people, and a great amount is left over.

2 Chronicles 31:10

When is too much, too much? It's safe to say human nature is to always want *more*. How do we balance what we want with what we need and can afford? How do we exercise self-restraint?

Jesus said, "To whom much is given, much is required,"³ but He did not say this to constrain our lifestyles. His direction is reflected in the Jerusalem elders' command to Paul in Galatians 2:10, which was to remember the poor—the very thing Paul intended to do.

To put it another way: whether we have much or little, we should remember the poor. Always. Today!

Ready or Not

> They did not labor in vain, nor will they bear children doomed to misfortune; for they will be a people *blessed* by the Lord, they and their descendants with them.
>
> **Isaiah 65:23**

In this passage, God spoke through His prophet Isaiah because the people were full of doubt. Their country was being invaded, and all but one of Israel's cities had been captured. Only Jerusalem remained. All of the prophets predicted doom, except Isaiah.

Then God showed up. Once again, in His mercy, He rescued His people.

Don't we all sometimes like to wallow in depression and self-doubt? "Pogo," a famous newspaper cartoon, once said, "We have met the enemy and he is us." This is true. Even so, God doesn't give us an easy way out. If Jesus had to pray and implore His Father, how much more should we, too?

Most of all, though, God wants us to believe. Believing in His power is the first step to *blessing*. Using His power in our lives is the next.

Ready to do that today?

Done Deal

> After Isaac had finished *blessing* him, and Jacob had scarcely left his father's presence, his brother Esau came in from hunting.
>
> **Genesis 27:30**

Have you ever wondered if you had done "this" instead of "that," how different your life would be? Maybe it would be a little different, maybe it would be dramatically different. Who knows?

Most people believe in luck. The concept of luck could be defined as a mysterious, invisible force that is supposed to affect everything, good and bad. Karma is luck's first cousin. Karma claims that by being good, we receive good things. If that were true, wouldn't all of us be rich and famous from all the wonderful "good deeds" we have done throughout our lives?

Our Biblical patriarch, Isaac, would strongly disagree with the concept of luck. He would call it God's will and a *blessing* instead.

God selected Jacob to receive the *blessing*. It was a done deal.

Bottom line? God doesn't believe in luck! He believes in *blessings*: look out for His blessings today.

No Place Like Home

Then the people left, each to his own home,
and David returned home to *bless* his family.
1 Chronicles 16:43

There's no place like home, right? The phrase "home sweet home" always makes it sound so warm and inviting. What if it isn't? What if, sometimes, it isn't the best place to go?

Going home when you are contemplating divorce isn't so sweet. It is a very stressful place when there is a cranky spouse or unappreciative child waiting for you every evening. Home can be very lonely too. David's home wasn't so great. In the chapter preceding this scripture, David's wife, Michal, saw him dancing for joy before the ark of the Lord and "despised him in her heart."

Not exactly the kind of welcome he was hoping for.

Bricks, wood, and roofing tiles keep the elements out, but that doesn't make a house a home. Regardless, whether our family keeps us warm or throws us out, it is good to remember: our only home is Heaven, and there is only one key to Heaven's giant pearl gate. That key is Jesus.

Use that Key to open your heart today.

Oil and Water

He created them male and female and *blessed* them. And when they were created He called them "man."

Genesis 5:2

Have you ever wondered why we need two kinds of people? Couldn't we be just as happy with only one sex? Doesn't it sometimes seem like God made a mistake, because truly, oil and water don't mix. Men and women are so different!

Pop quiz time! God made men and women so:

A.) He could have a good laugh
B.) He could keep us humble
C.) He knew we would need each other

Answer: *all* of the answers above are correct. Loving (or even liking) each other can be a daily challenge, but our relationship with Him is just like that too. Not from His end, but from ours. Familiarity doesn't breed contempt; instead, it breeds complacency. It is too easy to take others for granted.

Like any healthy marriage, God wants us to want an active, loving relationship with Him. He doesn't just want us to sit back and do *another* dinner and movie; He wants to dance! Dance with Jesus today.

Good and Bad

When the Lord your God has brought you into the land you are entering to possess, you are to proclaim on Mount Gerizim the *blessing*, and on Mount Ebal the curses.

Deuteronomy 11:29

Who doesn't like *blessings*? Bring 'em on, right? Curses, however, are another matter. Nobody wants to be cursed.

But what are curses anyway?

Usually, only witches in old movies utter curses, like *The Wizard of Oz's* infamous Wicked Witch of the West. But curses are mentioned many times in the Bible, so there must be more to it.

In this scripture, God is telling the Israelites if they worship false gods, bad things (curses) will happen to them. What does that have to do with us? Well, we worship false gods all the time: money, health, children, possessions, celebrities, ourselves, etc. Because of that, can bad things can happen to us, too?

The answer to that question is another question: will they today?

Howdy

Just then Boaz arrived from Bethlehem and greeted the harvesters, "The Lord be with you!" "The Lord *bless* you!" they called back.

Ruth 2:4

It's always nice to get a friendly greeting, isn't it? "How are you?" "Doing okay?" Whether the greeter really cares about how you are doing can often be questionable, though. Just like your response, right? "Fine, thanks." "Okay." "Not bad..."

No intimacy or genuinely shared feelings; we're just being polite.

How we greet God every day is much more important. We can be upbeat or ignore Him. Often, we grunt a quick prayer and move on. Yet we always want God to cheerfully grant our requests, right?

We have to understand He *loves* us, but He doesn't practice politeness. He is blunt, which is typically the way He gets our attention. When we feel that bluntness, it is good to remember that God didn't write a book on etiquette. He wrote one on obedience.

Be more genuine today.

One Last Shot

This is the *blessing* that Moses the man of God
pronounced on the Israelites before his death.
Deuteronomy 33:1

Moses's story is mostly one of rejection, frustration
and fear. Sound familiar? Still, just before he died, Moses *blessed* the very people who had made his life a living
hell for forty years.

Have you ever wanted to *finally* tell people off? Have
you ever just really wanted to let them know how badly
they have hurt, humiliated, or ignored you?

Moses put up with all that and more while living in
a desert for most of his life, serving the people of Israel
thanklessly, and never even stepping into the Promised
Land.

Not once did he curse his people. No, in spite of their
rebellious, difficult behavior, he *blessed* them.

Without God, it is impossible to *bless* people we really want to curse. If we can master that (and it takes a
lot of prayer), no one will be able to control us.

Our last shot today can and should always be a *blessing* for them.

Rest Assured

And God *blessed* the seventh day and made
it holy, because on it He rested from all the
work of creating that He had done.

Genesis 2:3

Did God really need to rest? It's a good question,
isn't it? Whether He needed to or not, the Bible tells us
clearly that He rested. If nothing else, this is a model set
for us since we need to rest too. But do we?

Weekends have replaced the concept of a Sabbath,
and our "Sabbaths" are often scheduled out to the last
minute. We definitely get tired, but we rarely rest. In
our ultra-competitive world, "rest" can even sound
wimpy.

The truth, however, is that God wants us to rest
because it gives us crucial time to enjoy Him and His
blessings. When we rest, we realize and appreciate the
many *blessings* God has given to us. It's also a measure
of faith: do we really trust Him to provide for us when
we aren't working? He has given us families, jobs, education, homes, cars, church communities, and much,
much more. He even has the future planned for us.

Rest assured of that today.

In and Out

You will be *blessed* when you come in and blessed when you go out.

Deuteronomy 28:6

God always knows when we're "in" with Him and when we're "out." It's the same with us: we're in with some people and out with others.

The problem is we're often in with those we know the least, like coworkers, and out with our families, and even ourselves!

Knowing God loves us, whether we're in or out with someone, or ourselves, is the great path to peace. We can approach everything with more joy and confidence. We are *blessed* by Him because *He loves us*, not because of who we are, or what we said or did, or didn't say or do.

Focusing on whether we're in or out with others is exhausting. We're out with God when we want to control our lives, and in with Him when we realize our dependence on Him for everything.

Staying in with God takes love. Love somebody better today.

Say Cheese!

All who see them will acknowledge that they
are a people the Lord has *blessed*.

Isaiah 61:9

Everybody smiles for the camera. Saying "cheese" widens the corners of our mouths, but how often do we genuinely smile at God? We've all been around someone who is so enthusiastic that it bugs us. Sometimes we want to slap them and make them embrace a more "realistic" view of life.

Yet, who is behaving more like Christ?

Christians ought to be the world's happiest people. God has a sense of humor, and since we're created in His image, we do too. Humor is God's way of humbling us, and helping us to never take ourselves too seriously. He knows what is best, and, if we really believed that, no one could wipe the smiles off our faces.

What do our faces look like when no one is watching? Shouldn't we be smiling?

After all, we are saved and headed for Heaven.

Be happy about that today.

Some Are, and Some Aren't

His children will be mighty in the land; the generation of the upright will be *blessed*.

Psalm 112:2

Every generation is concerned about the next. In the musical *Bye Bye Birdie*,[4] a father and a mother sing: "What's the matter with kids today?" It was written in the 1950s, so it goes to show—nothing has changed.

We were all kids. Now, we're in control and are, in our own way, mighty in the land; we're *blessed*. Yet the question is: "Are our children?"

The answer always seems to be that some are and some aren't. Does the fault lie in us for being less-than-perfect parents? God doesn't demand perfection, but He does demand progress, progress in our relationships, in our generosity, in our leadership, and in our love for Him.

Try to remember that uprightness has more to do with looking up and giving it up to Him and less to do with looking down and giving in to our flesh.

As this verse suggests, when we master this, our children will be *blessed*.

Mastering this will lead to a blessing today.

Guilty as Charged

But it will go well with those who convict the
guilty, and rich *blessing* will come upon them.
Proverbs 24:25

We all love to see justice carried out, don't we? Except, of course, when justice is about to be carried out
upon us. Convicting the guilty sounds simple: the first
question is whether the person is innocent, and the second is whether or not they could go free on a technical-
ity, even if they are guilty.

Yet, it is not as simple as it seems.

Once guilt is established, what is the appropriate
punishment? Spiritually speaking, without Jesus, it is
death and eternal separation from God, which is hell.
We are all guilty of sin. With Jesus, our guilt has been
laid upon Him, and we have been forgiven. We can't
forget, however, there are often serious ramifications
to sin this side of Heaven.

Forgiving a wrong doesn't mean the bad guys go
free; on the contrary, there are many Christian crimi-
nals in prisons. What it means is calling a sin "a sin,"
and accepting the consequences.

Only then can there be a plea for mercy, which God
can kindly grant today.

Go, Girl!

Most *blessed* of women be Jael, the wife of Heber the Kenite, most *blessed* of tent-dwelling women.

Judges 5:24

Women are often overlooked throughout history. The Bible, however, is full of courageous women who followed God and put the men around them to shame.

Take, for example, Jael, who drove a stake through the enemy commander's temple and won a war for Israel.

Today, godly women are fighting daily. They battle the sexualization of their daughters, their sisters, and themselves. They contend for the hearts and minds of their men and sons, trying desperately to shield them from the wicked explosion of pornography. They also continue to strive for appropriate recognition and respect.

Jael lived in a tent and saved her people; today, women contend with subtler and more sophisticated enemies. Regardless, Jesus is the new stake, and in the hand of a godly person, He'll win all the wars, too.

Are we willing to fight for Him today?

Expect the Unexpected

Then Balak's anger burned against Balaam.
He struck his hands together and said to him,
"I summoned you to curse my enemies, but
you have *blessed* them these three times."

Numbers 24:10

Life is unpredictable, isn't it? We plan, hope, and
pray, but we often don't get what we request. James
would say we don't receive because we doubt. He has
a point.

We ask but expect the worst. We usually think we're
not worthy of God's favor because we are sinners, and
we are; *however*, God gives rain to the righteous and the
wicked,⁵ so merit isn't in the picture. Balak paid Balaam
good money for him to curse Israel, but he only got
blessings upon Israel instead.

What if God wants us to *bless* somebody when everyone is cursing them? That would be unexpected.

That would be divine.

Be an unexpected blessing to someone today.

Forget Me Not

When you are harvesting in your field and overlook a sheaf, do not go back to get it. Leave it for the alien, the fatherless and the widow, so that the Lord your God may *bless* you in all the work of your hands.

Deuteronomy 24:19

We work hard, and it's very easy to suspect that those with less are lazy or made poor decisions; otherwise, they would have as much as we do, right?

Maybe not.

Job said men at ease have contempt for misfortune.[6] Yet the Lord is telling us we are called to be generous, whether we feel rich or not.

The man who left the sheaf may have had a poor harvest, but he still left it for those in even more need. When we do that—and, yes, sometimes it hurts—the Lord will *bless* us too.

Pray we won't forget those less fortunate today, too.

Hold On

Blessed are all who wait for Him.

Isaiah 30:18

Who likes waiting for anything? Red lights and traffic jams irritate us, and so do people who take forever in a checkout line. Waiting seems to waste our time because, in our culture, time is money, which means it is precious. All the tasks we have to squeeze into our ever-shrinking daily minutes show the immense value of our time.

Yet God wants us to wait for Him.

He doesn't have a watch or even a calendar. Not a great way to win a popularity contest, is it? Still, God knows what we want, and He decides whether we should have it.

Waiting on Him isn't wasting our time. God wants us to wait because He wants us to have faith and be dependent on Him.

We wait because God is not a vending machine—He is our Father. Treat Him like that today.

Staying Put

Stay in this land for a while, and I will be with you and will *bless* you.

Genesis 26:3

Staying in one home or job can mean stability if the people around us know and like us. God was calling Isaac to stay in a country in which he was a stranger. A land where his faith was to be hugely tested. God asked Isaac to stay in a bad situation with neighbors who were destroying his valuable wells.

He was free to leave at any time, but Isaac was faithful and stayed.

We all sometimes find ourselves in places or situations in which we are not appreciated or even feel threatened. We are free to leave too. Whether we should stay or go depends on God. He may be calling us to leave. It depends on what we perceive God wants us to do.

Knowing God's will always comes down to prayer and faith, not a desire for just momentary happiness today.

Once and For All

From the Lord comes deliverance. May Your
blessing be on your people.

Psalm 3:8

Don't we just love delivery services like Amazon?
Most of us also like to deliver good news, and we love it
when our favorite team delivers a victory, too.

But Biblical deliverance is different.

Biblical deliverance means to be rescued from some
bad incident or calamity. Unfortunately, we constantly
need deliverance because we are always sinning.

We sin when we silently mock someone older,
younger, fatter, or smaller. Whether it's someone less
intelligent, or anyone we disagree with, or someone
who doesn't look like us, we sin when we do not love,
and we usually only truly love people we like or those
who like us.

It's easy to dislike a lot of people, but deliverance is
God's way of saving us from ourselves. Jesus's death
didn't just deliver us from evil; He delivered us from
ourselves. From our selfishness.

Once and for all, starting today.

Landslide Victory

> This Melchizedek was the king of Salem and priest of God Most High. He met Abraham returning from the defeat of the kings and *blessed* him.
>
> **Hebrews 7:1**

God loves to *bless* us and does it so often, we either expect it or ignore it. We even like to believe we "create our own luck" by working hard and making smart decisions.

Yet, the Bible points to God's active involvement with us. He is not a puppeteer; instead, He is the great Conductor of our lives' symphonies.

Abraham knew this: he had been *blessed* by God beyond measure. Melchizedek *blessed* him too because of the great victory God gave Abraham. Abraham showed his gratitude by giving Melchizedek a tenth of everything he recovered from the enemy.

How can we show our thanks to Him for the victories we'll experience today?

Hero Worship

You are the most excellent of men and your
lips have been anointed with grace, since God
has *blessed* you forever.

Psalm 45:2

We sure love heroes, whether in real life or on the
big screen, but have you ever considered how heroes
make us both proud and envious? We all like to believe
we would be just as heroic if we were in the same situation, but in our heart, we know we might have chick-
ened out.

God is our great Hero. He protects us from the desires of our enemies, and they are much more ferocious
than we often know. Foes we don't recognize include
our egos, our greed, our pride, our lust, and just about
everything else that draws us away from God.

Even so, most heroes show up, fight, and then split.

God shows up, fights, and then *blesses* us.

In fact, it is His *blessing* that will help us act hero-
ically today.

Rest Stop

"Come, you who are *blessed* by the Lord," he
said. "Why are you standing here?"

Genesis 24:31

The word "come" invites us in. It welcomes us to
what we hope will be a restful place. The world is always
calling to us, beckoning with a huge smile to come and
join the party. Yet, the world is anything but restful.

God likewise calls us to come to Him, and there is
a huge difference between God's call and the world's.
Coming to God means we find true rest and peace; we
find acceptance and fulfillment. Acceptance *despite* our
failures. Fulfillment because we always seem to think
that we have to be earning our acceptance by "doing,"
even if it is without focus, as if being busy is an end
unto itself.

Coming to God is not a reprieve from the harshness
of the world, like being in the eye of the hurricane. Instead, it is a gentle, balmy, *consistent* breeze in the midst
of any brutal storm. It is peace in the middle of chaos. It
is continuous hope and happiness, and never despair.

So why are you just standing there? Go to God today!

Good Job

Moses inspected the work and saw that they
had done it just as the Lord had commanded.
So Moses *blessed* them.

Exodus 39:43

It feels good to accomplish something, doesn't it?
The satisfaction of knowing we've finished a project is
so rewarding. Imagine the thrill of completing the con-
struction of the Ark of the Covenant!

Yet Moses's *blessing* may have been as simple as
"good job." Nothing more needed to be said.

God wants us to do a good job, too. In Ephesians
2:10, Paul says we are called to do the good work God
has prepared for us in advance. Discovering what that
is can be overwhelming, but it is really pretty simple:
we're to master the art of loving our neighbor.

That is the Ark we're supposed to build now.

Let's try to do a good job of that today.

First, Second, Third

In that day Israel will be third, also with Egypt
and Assyria, a *blessing* on the earth.

Isaiah 19:24

Everybody wants to win. Finishing in third place has
almost no honor and is even more humiliating when
only three participants were in the race!

God put Israel in third place, behind his greatest enemies, to remind Israel that all of his success was from
Him and only Him. The Israelites wanted to take credit
for their achievements, but they continually forgot they
had no control over their future or past. Likewise, we
too tend to think we always pull ourselves up by our
bootstraps.

We don't, and when God shames us for our pride, it
is unforgettable. Let's always remember that.

One prayer we can pray today is for humility because
it is the one quality we all lack, all of the time.

Free Range

How *blessed* you will be, sowing your seed by every stream, and letting your cattle and donkeys range free.

Isaiah 32:20

Free-range chickens and eggs are a big deal these days. "Free-range" sounds so wild and open like the old West, doesn't it? But does God care that much about whether animals are penned up or range free?

The main lesson here is God wants us to be free in Christ.

After all, we get to choose our master. We can be slaves to our habits, faults, and prejudices, or we can serve the Holy One, Who set us free from sin by His death. "Freedom now!" was a cry of the civil rights movement. "Free at last!" can only be found in the Man who died to set us free.

Jesus is the fulfillment of Moses's prophetic mission, and if the Israelites were freed from slavery by Moses, we are freed from slavery through faith in Jesus.

And in Jesus, we can be free today!

Think It Through

*"The Lord *bless* you, my daughter," he replied.*
Ruth 3:10

In this verse, Boaz is *blessing* a woman who, in fact, is not his daughter. He is *blessing* a younger woman, Ruth, who had the courage to depend on God to change her future. Her future looked to be one of toil and poverty, yet she did not seek wealth. All she really wanted was to provide for her aged mother-in-law.

It's surprising how much Ruth loved her mother-in-law, Naomi. After losing her husband and both sons, Naomi was destitute. Thank God Ruth was selfless.

Many of us only think of God when we need something from Him. Like Naomi, we usually have nothing to offer Him, but like Ruth, we know that He still loves us and wants to care for us.

Ultimately, following Naomi's advice, Ruth was led to a wonderful new husband, Boaz.

Jesus wants to lead us to a new future in Him today.

Underwater

Take your flocks and herds, as you have said, and go. And also *bless* me.

Exodus 12:32

Moses told Pharaoh he wanted to take a three-day journey to sacrifice and worship the Lord. Pharaoh allowed it as long as Moses *blessed* him and asked God to remove the plague of flies.

Moses did, and God did.

Pharaoh knew he needed Moses's blessing because he was in over his head, yet shortly after this, he hardened his heart again.

When do we know we're underwater and in over our heads? When we start coughing from swallowing too much water? Sometimes God lets us go under the water, but only to make us aware of the depth of our mistakes.

Believing in Him is trusting He won't let us drown. When we rely on Him, we can swim in the deep end where His big kids play. We will know that He will save us yet again today.

FEBRUARY 11

Home Sweet Home

The ark of the Lord remained in the house of
Obed-Edom the Gittite for three months, and
the Lord *blessed* him and his entire household.

2 Samuel 6:11

As we all know, most people believe in luck. Some
carry lucky charms or wear lucky clothes. Athletes often
have their "good luck" rituals before they compete. Lot-
teries and casinos thrive on the idea of luck, but in reality, there is no magic force that helps us win.

Obed-Edom didn't believe in luck, but He did believe in God, and God *blessed* him abundantly because
he took the Ark into his home. Even more praiseworthy
is that he took the Ark into his home right after another
man had been struck dead for mishandling it.

Obed-Edom had faith, yet faith can be vague and
scary. We don't know the future; we only know that
God loves us and can be trusted.

When we act in faith today, even if we mishandle
something, we won't be struck down. Instead, we'll be
blessed.

Bless You, My Child

Then Saul said to David, "May you be *blessed*,
my son David; you will do great things and
surely triumph."

1 Samuel 26:25

Nobody likes to admit a mistake. Here, Saul knew
he had messed up. Earlier in the chapter, Saul asked for
forgiveness from David, even though he'd been trying
to kill him. Saul *blesses* him here because David spared
his life a second time.

It is easy to bash Saul, but he really isn't given much
credit here. He was the king, and as misguided as he
was, he saw David as a potential enemy.

Yet Saul knew he was beaten.

Why?

Saul *blessed* David because he knew David was
innocent.

Do we *bless* our enemies? How about cursing them?
We're really good at that, aren't we? Saul was an imperfect person who knew when he was beaten by a more
godly person.

When is it time to give in and bless your enemies?
How about today?

Such a Deal

The Lord protects and preserves them—they are counted among the *blessed* in the land—He does not give them over to the desire of their foes.

Psalm 41:2

Running scared is an awful way to live. In modern society, there are plenty of things to be frightened of: diseases, volatile stock markets, terrorists, crime, illness, aging, accidents, etc. We buy insurance to cover some of our risks, hire experts to help us avoid others, and pray God takes care of the rest!

God certainly doesn't discourage us from being prudent, but He's the only ultimate safety net. This verse refers to His protection of those who have shown kindness to the weak. God always encourages us to help the helpless because when we do, He's "got our back" against everyone, *especially* our enemies, whether those are real or imagined.

That is such a deal!

God will reward us for every kind act done to someone less *blessed* than us.

So how can you help the helpless today?

Thanks, Mom

Then the mother said, "The Lord *bless* you, my son!"

Judges 17:2

One common denominator for all mankind is we are all born with mothers. As adults, some of us have the joy of having older mothers; sometimes, though, this can be an irritation, as many older mothers find it hard to stop mothering. Even so, an encouraging word from mom can make your day, while a rebuke can spoil it.

The mother in today's scripture is *blessing* her son for returning the money he stole from her. Only a mom could do that.

This woman was old, and oldness is a new disease; it's like a modern virus no one wants, but throughout history, all have been destined to catch it. Still, enjoying our elders as we become like them can be a challenge.

If we could only approach old age as a mother does, we could learn to appreciate everyone and forgive anybody for anything.

What a *blessing* that would bring today.

Listen Up

When such a person hears the words of the oath, he invokes a *blessing* on himself and therefore thinks, 'I will be safe, even though I persist in going my own way.' This will bring disaster on the watered land as well as the dry.

Deuteronomy 29:19

"Free" sounds great: free money, free love, and free speech. Total freedom sounds too good to be true, and it almost always is.

Jesus said the truth you know will set you free. He set many free while He was on Earth: lepers, cripples, tax collectors, sinners, and many more. Unfortunately, the man in this verse thinks if he checks the right boxes, he'll be free, too.

Listen up! Jesus gives us freedom in exchange for love—love for His Father and others. Nothing is really free. He paid the price for us with His life.

What price are we willing to pay today?

Soften Up

You drench its furrows and level its ridges;
you soften it with showers and *bless* its crops.
Psalm 65:10

Soft things are usually very appealing. Soft pillows, soft mattresses, and soft sheets conjure up the thought of a restful night's sleep. Even being called an "old softie" can be a compliment.

Soft is not always good, though. Being soft on crime is usually a criticism.

In this Psalm, God is praised for softening the soil with rain. Rain is almost always used in the Bible as a *blessing* from God. It is His way of reminding us we are fully dependent on Him for even the most basic needs.

Some people accuse others of praying for trivial things. But God wants us to pray for it all: from the essential to the elaborate.

God wants us to soften Him up by praying for everything. Cast all your cares upon Him because He cares for you.[7]

Go ahead and ask for anything and everything today.

Lying Eyes

They fully intended to topple him from his lofty place; they delight in lies. With their mouths they *bless*, but with their hearts they curse.

Psalm 62:4

Honesty can be hard. It is often easier to flatter our way to acceptance. We all have to admit that fibbing, or even "shading" the truth, are mechanisms we use to get people to like us. This is still lying, though. As a result, we rarely know whether someone is being honest or feeding us just enough flattery to keep us happy.

And most people really don't like the truth, even though it would set them free.

God is trustworthy. He doesn't need us to like Him. God is honest, sometimes brutally so. He wants us to walk in love, and lying is not loving in any way.

We don't have to be brutally honest all, or even most, of the time. We just need to be real today, and trust that those who surround us are playing it straight, too.

Hide and Seek

Then the Lord said, "Shall I hide from Abraham what I am about to do? Abraham will surely become a great and powerful nation, and all nations on earth will be *blessed* through him."

Genesis 18:17-18

Abraham was intelligent and optimistic. Still, he may have believed his nephew, Lot, was smart to select the well-watered Jordan valley as his portion of what later became Israel. Did he regret allowing Lot first choice on where to settle?

After all, Lot chose to settle in Sodom, and Sodom and its sister city, Gomorrah, were both vibrant cities. What could go wrong?

Things go wrong all the time. We guess, estimate, and approximate; we play the odds and take our chances. We take risks at work, with our investments, and even driving home in traffic, but we cannot see the future. As we know, Lot's choice definitely went wrong.

Abraham's only risk was trusting God. God doesn't play hide and seek. He just wants us to seek Him.

Our only risk is not seeking Him today.

Singled Out

At that time the Lord set apart the tribe of Levi to carry the ark of the covenant of the Lord, to stand before the Lord to minister and pronounce *blessings* in His name, as they still do today.

Deuteronomy 10:8

Getting singled out can be a mixed bag; while being singled out for praise or for an achievement is wonderful, it's not so great when it is for a blunder.

The Levites were singled out as God's priestly tribe because of their loyalty to Him. For example, when the Israelites began worshiping the golden calf, the Levites stepped in to defend God's honor.

The Levites understood *blessing* the people was a very special privilege.

We also are singled out to bless people, especially those we don't like: co-workers, bosses, family members, even strangers.

Blessing people we don't like can be very tough, yet Jesus died on a cross for them, too.

Which is harder?

Let's try harder to single out someone for a blessing today.

Fat and Sassy

Then Joshua *blessed* them and sent them home.

Joshua 22:6

A land of milk and honey sounds too good to be true. The thought conjures up blissful images of green pastures, babbling brooks, and balmy breezes; add to that tables overflowing with food, surrounded by happy people. That is exactly the home God gave the Israelites after they had spent forty years in the desert; it was completely furnished with houses, gardens, and vineyards.

Sadly, they quickly forgot the *blessing* was from God; they got fat and sassy.

We often get fat and sassy, too. We take God's *blessings* for granted and envy those who seem to have more than us. Our milk and honey is our family, our friends, our work, our health, and our relationship with Jesus.

Even if one or more of those goes sour for a moment, God's love remains sweet.

And we didn't have to live forty years in a desert to get it. We can taste His blessings today.

All or Nothing

I will bless those who *bless* you.

Genesis 12:3

Most of us ask God for health and wealth, but what else do we ask for? Fame looks like it would be fun. What about power? Being in a position to solve all of the world's problems, or at least some of them, sounds rewarding.

So, why don't we get those things? Why are our lives so often frustrating, even futile?

In this scripture, God was telling Abraham to move to another country where he knew no one, much like modern missionaries do. Abraham went because he believed God's promise to bless him. And God did.

We all want God to *bless* us as He did Abraham, but we rarely want to obey Him to such a degree.

James says, "Show me your faith without deeds, and I'll show you my faith by what I do."[8]

What are we doing today? Nothing? Anything? Everything?

FEBRUARY 22

Finders Keepers

Blessed is the man who finds wisdom, the man
who gains understanding.

Proverbs 3:13

Finding a treasure map marked with an X or a secret
passageway that conceals hoards of gold sounds as tan-
talizing as it does improbable. We're just happy when
we find something we've lost, especially if it's valuable.

Solomon applies this principle to wisdom. Wisdom
and understanding are the most extraordinary discov-
eries; in Proverbs alone, Solomon mentions wisdom
over *fifty* times! Wisdom is one of the most effective
ways we can draw close to God on this side of Heaven.

Biblical wisdom is God sharing His understanding
with us. That is what makes it so precious.

Solomon also said the fear of the Lord is the beginning of wisdom.[9] This fear doesn't mean we need to be
afraid; it means we need to show God the reverence
we have for our superiors. And God is our ultimate
Superior.

All true wisdom comes from God, and He wants us
to pray for more of it today.

So What?

And Abraham said to God, "If only Ishmael might live under Your *blessing!*"

Genesis 17:18

The Bible and the Koran have completely different stories about Ishmael. Ishmael is Abraham's firstborn son in both, but in the Bible, Abraham shows his obedience when God chooses Isaac, not Ishmael, as Abraham's heir. The Koran replaces Isaac with Ishmael as Abraham's heir, and Ishmael is to be sacrificed by Abraham, not Isaac.

Many people would say, "So what?" The "what" is that God answered Abraham's prayer; He *blessed* Ishmael. God gave him twelve sons, and Ishmael became very powerful. This reminds us God can *bless* whoever He wants, even though it can be irritating when He is kind to someone we don't like. He still sends rain on the righteous and the wicked.

Mohammad got it totally wrong, but the facts remain true. God blessed Abraham for his obedience, and He'll *bless* us for ours today, too.

Get to Work

So that the Lord your God may *bless* you in all
the work of your hands.

Deuteronomy 14:29

Work, work, work! Everybody has to do it. Some
people say that you should find your passion, while others demand workers' rights. Toil is a synonym for work;
so is labor. Work is usually not fun, otherwise, it would
be called recreation.

Yet, we all want our work to be meaningful, and we
want God to *bless* it.

Did you know God can give us both? He can give
our work immense significance and *blessing*, regardless of the job or role in the company. Christian history
is filled with saints who had menial jobs but enriched
thousands whose lives they touched.

Making work worthwhile takes Jesus. His job is to
bring people to His Father. It is our job too. Yet how we
handle ourselves at work is much more powerful than
what we say or preach.

A phrase commonly attributed to St. Francis of Assi-
si says it best: "Preach the gospel at all times. Use words
if necessary." Let's get to work mastering that today.

Fountain of Youth

May your fountain be *blessed*, and may you rejoice in the wife of your youth.

Proverbs 5:18

Fountains are fantastic: watching the water cascade and hearing the sound of its splashing. Fountains are peaceful places for rest and reflection, and for many cities, they help define their character and soul.

Solomon's focus in this verse is faithfulness. He understood the devastation adultery can have on the family fountain, its character and soul. Those temptations were not new in his time, and the same ones infect ours, too. Being married can become routine, and complacency is a dangerous enemy. The spouse of our youth grows old, and it is tempting to allow the fountain to dry up.

Whether it's physical adultery or the emotional variety that Jesus cautioned us against, what we should fear is sin and dying separated from Him.

This, of course, can never happen if we're constantly filled with His Spirit, the never-ending fountain of living water.[10]

Pray today that He will let us drink deeply of that water and not be lead into temptation.

Making Memories

The memory of the righteous is a *blessing*, but the name of the wicked will rot.

Proverbs 10:7

Everyone desires to be remembered for something good. It may be the joyful memory of playtimes that a grandchild will cherish. It may be a more tangible accomplishment like raising funds for a community in need, or it could even be our personality that leaves a void with others when we're gone. Obituaries serve that purpose.

Not all memories of us will be good, however, because we're not all that good. We're human, and we are very often self-centered, short-tempered, and insecure. As Jesus observed, even the wicked love those who love them.[11]

What makes us good is God.

He has infused us with the Holy Spirit to guide us, prompt us and inspire us. As Christians, we are commanded by Jesus to love those we cannot stand (and who can't stand us!)

Accomplishing that today would make us truly memorable.

Safe and Secure

But King Solomon will be *blessed*, and David's throne will remain secure before the Lord forever.

1 Kings 2:45

We are all growing toward old age, whether we admit it or not. It usually takes turning fifty before mortality starts sinking in. When it does, time feels much shorter, and what we do with it seems much more important.

In this verse, Solomon had just become king and was living in the shadow of his deceased father, the great King David. Everyone was watching to see whether young Solomon could measure up.

Solomon prayed for help, but specifically for wisdom to lead God's people well. God answered his prayer and richly rewarded him.

Solomon believed wisdom is the principal thing,[12] yet we don't have to be old to be wise. James says all we have to do is ask for it in faith, and God will give us wisdom liberally.[13] Instead, we usually ask for health and wealth. If we want it all, including a secure throne for our family, let's pray for wisdom, which is ultimately seeking God's kingdom above all else.[14]

God will take care of the rest today.

Cover Up

Blessed is the one whose transgressions are
forgiven, whose sins are covered.

Psalm 32:1

"Cover-up" can mean many different things. It can
mean something sinister like corruption in politics. It
can mean the cover-ups women wear when they are
sunbathing beside the pool in their swimsuits. Hiding
things from view is the general idea.

In this verse, "cover-up" means our sins being made
invisible to God.

Although He knows all things, He deliberately chooses not to see the sins of those who are saved in Christ.
In fact, in Isaiah 43:25, God says our sins are blotted
out, which means He doesn't even remember them.

The very reason Jesus died was to cover up our rebellious acts toward His Father. When rebels are caught,
the penalty is usually death. Our situation is no exception, except Jesus paid the price for us with His own
life. It is important to realize this is much more than
a "get out of jail free" card; it is God hitting the delete
button, over and over again.

To receive this mind-blowing *blessing*, all we have to
do is believe. Instantly, God will cover up our faults and
give us an increase in faith today.

Last Call

...and they will call him *blessed*.

Psalm 72:17

This psalm was written by Solomon, the wise king and son of David. He wrote it to describe how a good king should rule, and some would say he is also describing how the Messiah will reign. The Messiah is Jesus.

But do we act like Jesus is our Messiah, or do we take that for granted? Today, is there anything in our lives that would be so distinctive that someone would say without hesitation that we are Christians? Probably not. We tend to want to be "private" in our personal lives because we either do not want to draw attention to ourselves, or we are afraid of negative fallout.

But Jesus called us to put our lamps on stands so that everyone can see His light. We have been gifted with an extra day this year, so with these extra 24 hours let's make it our goal to be more like Him, to act more like Him and to show others we belong to Him.

New Year's resolutions typically start on January 1. Let's start this one today, on Leap Day!

The Sixth Sense

Taste and see that the Lord is good; *blessed* is
the one who takes refuge in Him.

Psalm 34:8

Our five senses are sight, hearing, touch, smell and
taste. Taste and smell are minimized by the other three,
but they are critical to the one thing vital for life: food.

We can go through life blind, deaf, and paralyzed,
but not tasting can lead to malnutrition and potentially
death.

God is tasty. He can be salty, but usually, He's sweet.
On occasion (when we've done something to require it),
He can be bitter and sour. What flavor He shares var-
ies, which is why we are so dependent on Him. We only
pray for the sweet, but growth tends to come when we
sting from the salt.

While we deserve a steady diet of bitterness, the
Lord is good. He wants us to enjoy our relationship
with Him—that is the sixth sense.

Taste and see the goodness of the Lord today!

Hang in There

I will send you such a *blessing* in the sixth year
that the land will yield enough for three years.
Leviticus 25:21

Faith can be some tough stuff! There are experiments where participants are blindfolded and led around by people with sight. What they found was the sense of dependency can be overwhelming.

The same is true of our relationship with God. In this verse, God required His people to not farm for a full year, every seventh year, as a way to let the land rest. He promised to give them enough in the sixth year to feed them through the seventh year, as long as they were obedient. Waiting on God for our entire sustenance every seven years would be unnerving, regardless of the strength of our faith.

No crops can mean starvation, but that's what God commanded, and He was serious.

What do we do to deliberately demonstrate our faith? Usually nothing. Tithing helps because giving ten percent each month adds up. What about more? God doesn't care about our net worth; He cares about our faith.

This verse tells us if we have faith and we act on it, we are sure to receive a *blessing*.

What's the return on investment for a *blessing*?

Ask God! He wants to show you today.[15]

Double Trouble

Blessed is the one who always trembles before God, but whoever hardens their heart falls into trouble.

Proverbs 28:14

Trembling is a sign of either physical weakness or emotional fragility. We never tremble when we feel strong and self-assured. God wants us to approach Him confidently,[16] but never in our own assurance. We can never feel strong and confident in our own strength before God.

Instead, we are to honor God to such a degree that we tremble before His holiness in humility and worship.

But we often think we don't need God, so we don't tremble before Him. We're not afraid because we think we are strong enough to control our own life.

This is how we become hardened.

Trouble soon follows since we have no external brake; we don't acknowledge or seek the Holy Spirit to prompt us or push us back onto the right path.

Trembling or trouble. Pick one today.

Beg, Borrow or Steal

For the Lord your God will *bless* you as He has
promised, and you will lend to many nations
but borrow from none.

Deuteronomy 15:6

Credit cards are a marvelous invention. With a high
enough credit limit, we can buy almost anything, and
there is some security in that. If handled correctly, a
credit card can be a wonderful convenience; if poorly
managed, they can result in crushing debt. Paying off
a card takes tremendous discipline, and the creditor always has the upper hand. They can sue, foreclose and
garnish. Bankruptcy awaits if repayments aren't taken
seriously.

God promised the Israelites they would be the lend-
ers and in control if they followed His laws. He guaranteed them they would flourish and would never need to
borrow.

The only condition was they had to follow His laws.

They didn't, of course, and most of us still don't. And
the results are still predictable.

Ultimately, we either love God and others, or we try
to beg, borrow or steal any sense of peace we can find.

Make the right choice today.

Larger-Than-Life

When God made His promise to Abraham, since there was no one greater than Him to swear by, He swore by Himself, saying, "I will surely *bless* you and give you many descendants." And so after waiting patiently, Abraham received what was promised.

Hebrews 6:13-15

We love identifying with people who are larger-than-life, whether it's a movie star, a top athlete, or a particular politician. We want to be like them, and we tend to overlook any of their flaws because it doesn't serve our purpose.

Even though we're the apple of His eye,[17] God doesn't kid Himself. He knows everything about us: our flaws, our shortcomings, our frustrations, and our sins.

Abraham wasn't perfect either, but he had faith. Despite his flaws, he learned to wait patiently.

It's always the waiting that gets us, isn't it? It is one thing to believe, but another to maintain faith over many decades.

If you want to identify with anyone, why not Abraham? Our waiting in faith will always be rewarded, either here or there.

Pray it will be today.

Risky Business

Blessed and holy are those who have a part in
the first resurrection.

Revelation 20:6

We live on the edge, don't we? It's not just when
we're driving in traffic that puts us at risk; our habits,
thoughts, and attitudes often get us into trouble, too.

Taking calculated risks, like investing our money
or changing jobs for a better future, can be beneficial.
When God calls on us to take big risks for Him, though,
we often shrink back due to a fear of rejection or a lack
of faith.

The book of Revelation says the only people who will
have a part in the first resurrection were those who
had been beheaded for Christ! That's a bigger deal than
sharing the gospel with a co-worker, isn't it? While the
risks we take today won't lead to decapitation, they
might lead to rejection.

What risks are you willing to run today?

Trading Places

Eli would *bless* Elkanah and his wife, saying, "May the Lord give you children by the woman to take the place of the one she prayed for and gave to the Lord."

1 Samuel 2:20

Here's how we want a vow to work: we have a big problem, and we need God's help, so we try to make a deal with Him. But God makes promises, not deals, despite how much we wish He did.

Here, Elkanah's wife, Hannah, promised God that if He gave her a child, she would devote it to God. God *blessed* her, not because of any "deal" she was trying to make, but because she promised to devote the child to God *when* it was born. She was blessed because she had the faith God would grant her request.

The prophet Samuel was this child, born to Hannah and Elkanah.

The only vow God consistently honors is a vow of devotion to love and serve Him. Hannah knew that, and now, today, so do we.

Eat, Drink and Be Merry

I will *bless* her with abundant provisions; her
poor I will satisfy with food.

Psalm 132:15

Eating is essential. You might have heard the saying
"life eats life," which explains that everything alive eats
something. Even plants use up the soil.

People eat for more than just nutrition; we eat so-
cially, too. Meal times are often the only time in our day
we relax enough to talk, joke, and share. God could have
created us without the need to eat, but He didn't because He wanted us to communicate and share.

In this scripture, like many others, the poor are honored because they're the most dependent upon God.
Praying hard for daily bread is humbling, and although
God is in charge and never fails, nobody likes being
humbled.

Eat, drink, and be merry in humility today, and
thank God for it.

Name Game

He *blessed* them that day and said, "In your name will Israel pronounce these *blessings*: May God make you like Ephraim and Manasseh."

Genesis 48:20

Names used to mean something. Someone named "Smith," for example, was a blacksmith, and a person named "Cooper" was a barrel maker. Today, names don't carry special status unless we're related to someone famous. In the Bible, however, the family's name identified a person's tribe and clan. Ephraim and Manasseh, for example, were Joseph's children, but they were adopted by their grandfather Jacob, who gave them a special *blessing*.

God *blesses* us, not for what we do—because we're always going to sin—but because of family lineage, too. We're adopted into God's family when we first call Him our Father and Jesus our Brother and Lord.

While we may not inherit any wealth from our Earthly family, we know our inheritance from our Father is just Heavenly!

Try to find ways to bring others into God's family today.

See You Later

Early in the morning Laban kissed his grandchildren and his daughters and *blessed* them.
Then he left and returned home.

Genesis 31:55

Nobody likes saying goodbye forever. We go through
all kinds of excuses to pretend a separation is only temporary. We say "until we meet again," or "see you later,"
or "until next time." We like to show optimism, even
when we sometimes know it is the last encounter.

In this scripture, Laban knew this was the end. He
would never see his daughters or his grandchildren
again because of how he had treated Jacob.

It hurt deeply.

For most of us, however, we usually don't know
when it will be the last time we see someone. People
come and go from our lives quickly, and they're often
not only mobile but sadly dispensable, as well.

Thankfully, God said He'll never leave us, nor for-
sake us.[18]

With God, it's never over. Today is always a new
beginning.

Good to Great

I will make you into a great nation, and I will
bless you.

Genesis 12:2

What is the definition of great? Is it having unlimited wealth? Is it having power, influence, or fame? Is it as simple as being a wonderful spouse, or parent, or friend?

In this scripture, Abraham was promised greatness because of his unwavering faith. Most of us, however, have faith until the first sign of failure. Then we excuse our unbelief by blaming time, space, and other people.

It is also important to understand that fame is different from greatness. Fame is fleeting. Greatness endures. Like Abraham, we'll only achieve greatness by being faithful to God's will for our life.

Abraham's journey from good to great was not easy. Neither is ours.

But with unwavering faith and devotion to God's plan, we can start achieving greatness today.

Turn, Turn, Turn

Our God, however, turned the curse into a blessing.

Nehemiah 13:2

Aren't we so relieved when things turn out much better than we expected? Many of us are so glad we didn't marry that person we thought we were in love with. Some of us thought a job loss was a catastrophe until it led to a bigger opportunity. Maybe it was even a health issue that forced a much-needed change.

It has been said that "God writes in straight lines with crooked letters." This means He knows where He's taking us and how long the journey will last, but the frustrations we face are His way of continually turning us back in the right direction. It's like driving: we change lanes and make turns, but we're moving toward our destination.

Sometimes, we may even feel lost, but God is never lost. He's really driving the car.

Be obedient, look out the windows, feel the bumps and try to enjoy the view today.

Screw-up

The woman gave birth to a boy and named him Samson. He grew and the Lord *blessed* him.

Judges 13:24

Samson was the first child of a previously barren couple. After much anguish and prayer, one day, an angel appeared and announced they'd have a son. The angel gave very specific instructions for his upbringing. Samson's parents obeyed, but for whatever reason, Samson had some major screw-ups, right up until the very end of his life.

Parents usually try to nurture their children in the best way possible; sometimes it works, sometimes it doesn't. Emotional maturity is a slow, painful process that typically improves with age. This is not always the case with spiritual maturity. Most Christians know what to do; we just don't do it.

We, too, are screw-ups.

Age isn't guaranteed to help, only reading scripture and prayer are.

The good news? God forgives us when we fail.

The bad news? We sometimes have a hard time forgiving ourselves.

Let's try that today.

All You Can Eat

Nevertheless, you may slaughter your animals in any town and eat as much of the meat as you want, as if it were a gazelle or deer, according to the *blessing* the Lord your God gives you.

Deuteronomy 12:15

Many people love all-you-can-eat restaurants. "Keep it coming!" is the motto, and it's only when it is over that they are stuffed and uncomfortable (then they regret that third piece of pie!).

One of the few things we usually want less of is when we're commanded to love people we don't like—but God wants to feed us with humility, not insincerity.

Much like an all-you-can-eat buffet, Jesus wants to fill us up with love for His Father and others, to the point where we can't walk, we can only waddle!

We can only do this by spending time with Him in prayer, scripture reading, and church attendance.

Once we digest that, we'll appreciate the One who set the example by loving us when we weren't very lovable.

Eat up every crumb of His blessings today.

Bear Fruit

God *blessed* them and said, "Be fruitful and increase in number; fill the earth and subdue it..."

Genesis 1:28

In real estate, the three most important things are location, location, location! For most of us, the three most important things in our lives are control, control, control. We want to control *every* aspect of our lives: financial, social, and emotional.

God is far better qualified for controlling our lives, though. He wants us to listen to Him for direction on *everything* because becoming fruitful isn't a suggestion, it's a command. He wants us to bear fruit by spreading His word and love to others.

Bear in mind this does not mean having children, it's about making disciples.

Making disciples can be scary. Nobody likes rejection, but Jesus was rejected far more than we will ever be. God has ultimate control, but realizing this and being submissive to Him takes humility.

Submitting to His will requires faith and obedience. Do we have enough of it today?

Right on Target

Blessed is the man whose quiver is full of them.
They will not be put to shame when they contend with their enemies in the gate.

Psalm 127:5

Quivers hold arrows, and arrows are weapons. They can be used offensively or defensively. Many of us only think of using lethal force defensively; we wouldn't harm anyone unless they were a threat to ourselves or our family.

But King David used offensive weapons almost exclusively.

We should too.

The culture dominates us. We don't want to offend, but that's really an excuse for not wanting to get shot down. We don't like being embarrassed. We're wimps. Solomon says here that our children (who are compared to arrows in a quiver) won't be shamed when they make a stand, however forceful or gentle that stand may be.

God has filled our quiver with all sorts of arrows. He wants us to aim, go on the offensive and start making a greater difference today!

Go the Distance

> But if that place is too distant and you have
> been *blessed* by the Lord your God and cannot
> carry your tithe...
>
> **Deuteronomy 14:24**

Tithing from what we earn is not easy. Making a contribution by writing a check, transferring funds, or charging a credit card is a physical step we have to take. This brings home the reality of giving ten percent of our income away to the work of the Lord.

As we think about making that gift, it can suddenly seem extravagant, too large a sacrifice or even unnecessary.

We convince ourselves that others will help, that we need the money for "more important" things this month, or that we'll get to it later.

God isn't unreasonable; He's practical. In this verse, He knew that transporting sheep long distances to the temple was difficult and often dangerous. God said the Israelites could sell those and bring the earnings instead.

But they had to do it, whether their harvest was good or bad, whether their family was healthy or sick.

Go the distance means, "trust and obey, there's no other way,"—*today*!

Walk on the Wild Side

Blessed are all who fear the Lord, who walk in His ways.

Psalm 128:1

Shouldn't we love God, not fear Him? Doesn't He love us? Fear sounds negative since it's the opposite of love, right? It is understandable that God can seem scary since we can't see, smell, or touch Him, yet He's supposed to control every aspect of our lives.

Still, this is not the type of fear God wants us to have of Him.

Fearing God means we revere Him; He is almighty, right! Because of His patience, though, He'd rather *bless* us than curse us. That's why walking with Him is such a wild journey. We normally don't walk on the wild side of life, it's too nerve-wracking; however, God invites us to walk with Him even though we're frightened.

That's radical. And the only thing holding us back from radical living is a lack of faith.

Instead of being fearful, start walking with Him and see what amazing adventures await today.

Heaven Help Us

May you be *blessed* by the Lord, the Maker of heaven and earth.

Psalm 115:15

Making something always has a sense of accomplishment to it (unless we're making a mess!). Some people crochet, others refurbish cars, and still, others grow fantastic tomatoes. God is the Master builder, and He created everything without our help. He can always find someone else to get His will done if we're disobedient.

Unfortunately, the bottom line is we always need His help.

Yet even in our obedience, we make messes and mistakes all the time. Even when He *blesses* us, it doesn't mean we'll never fail again. In fact, one of God's *blessings* is He'll always forgive our shortcomings and inadequacies, as long as we are willing to confess our sins and ask for His help.

And He loves to be asked for help.

Saint Gregory said, "We pay God a compliment by praying for great things."

Pray for great things today.

Skill Set

Bless all his skills, O Lord, and be pleased with
the work of his hands.

Deuteronomy 33:11

Pleasing God can be both easy and difficult, but because He's our Father, He loves us, and He's always willing to forgive us, even when it seems tough to please Him. He corrects us, just like most of our parents did.

Good parents have the skillset of being firm with their children when necessary but never abusive. Their goal is to simply teach their children right from wrong.

Right in God's eyes is loving Him and everyone else. Wrong is ignoring Him and the others we choose to ignore.

Becoming skilled at our work takes time, education, and attitude. God put us here to work. What we do isn't as important as being thankful for our work, anyone who is unemployed knows that.

God will bless our work if we ask Him. As our loving Father, He'll probably *bless* it even if we forget to ask.

Remember to ask Him to *bless* it today.

Bitter Sweet

Bless those who curse you, pray for those who
mistreat you.

Luke 6:28

It's human nature to be nice to people who are nice
to us. Waiters and clerks are trained to be nice to us,
which is why we treat them better than people we are
supposed to love.

Friends and family are supposed to be honest with
us, but when it comes to warm and fuzzy emotions,
niceness beats honesty any day!

Still, in this verse, Jesus asks us to do the impossible.
Mean people deserve to be treated with contempt, don't
they? Apparently, Jesus missed that memo. He asked
His Father to forgive the very people who were crucify-
ing Him. He didn't even curse those who whipped Him;
He remained silent.

What do we get when we *bless* the hateful people?

God's peace. The peace that He promised all who believe His words.

Revenge sounds sweet, but it always results in
bitterness.

Today choose love. Today choose peace.

Fear Factor

Thus is the man *blessed* who fears the Lord.

Psalm 128:4

Fear means one of two things: fright or respect. God doesn't need to frighten us; plenty of other things do. We're fearful of failure, rejection, and all manner of financial, family and work issues. Some people are afraid for our country, while others worry about their health. We never seem to run out of things to fret about.

Respect, on the other hand, is vague. We are told to respect police officers, parents, and bosses, but we're not really sure why, other than the fact that they occupy an office of authority. God, too, wants us to fear Him because of the office He occupies, yet He is entirely worthy of His role. As Almighty *God*, He created us and ultimately deserves our recognition and appreciation, while we tend to believe we made it all by ourselves.

Today let's not forget to acknowledge that we owe it *all* to Him.

Today don't be afraid of God; be fearful for those who don't know Him.

Free Delivery

"And *blessed* be God Most High who delivered
your enemies into your hand." Then Abram
gave him a tenth of everything.

Genesis 14:20

God is a *big* God. The Lord's prayer says, "deliver us
from evil." He also delivers us from stupidity and self-
satisfaction. We always think we've got things under
control, only to discover we've painted ourselves into a
corner.

In this verse, Abraham had just won a great battle.
He didn't have the strongest army, but he did have God.
God delivered him without asking for anything in return. God's deliverance was free, no strings attached.
Abraham showed gratitude by giving Melchizedek a
tenth of everything. As God's priest, Melchizedek could
accept that token of thanksgiving.

God's deliverance is free of charge, all day long. It
may not be a victory in a huge battle, but it may be a victory over a tough temptation.

Free is good! Always go to God. Always show Him
your constant gratitude today.

Pour It On

For I will pour water on the thirsty land, and streams on the dry ground. I will pour out My Spirit on your off-spring, and My *blessings* on your descendants.

Isaiah 44:3

Water symbolizes life, but it's much more than symbolic. We will die without water. Even becoming dehydrated can cause problems. We usually need more water than what we consume.

We can also experience emotional and spiritual dehydration from the stresses of life; our souls and minds cry out for relief.

The Bible uses the concept of water over and over again to represent God's relationship with us. We'll die without Him. He knows that, and we have to learn it.

Once we sincerely ask Him for help, He will not only quench our thirst, He will flood us, and those we love, with peace and hope.

Jesus said that the water He gives provides eternal life. Let's drink to that today!

The Life of the Party

For seven days celebrate the Feast of the Lord your God at the place the Lord will choose. For the Lord will *bless* you in all your harvest and in all the work of your hands, and your joy will be complete.

Deuteronomy 16:15

God loves celebrations. Three times each year, He commanded His people to come and rejoice in His *blessings*, each feast lasting seven whole days! These celebrations always started and ended with an acknowledgment that everything the people had received came from Him. He wants to be the life of the party.

Our harvests depend entirely on Him too, and, as we know, some harvests are more abundant than others. Yet whether they are big or small, we need to celebrate His kindness, provision, and mercy with joy!

God blesses us abundantly and far more than we deserve. We honor God by thanking Him, and what better way to do that than by giving a party in His honor!

Pray for a joyful and fun-filled day today.

Having It All

Her children will call her *blessed*; her husband also, and he praises her.

Proverbs 31:28

Being a mother and wife has never been easy. Historically, many children died in infancy, and a mother's death during childbirth used to be all too frequent. Back then, if a woman survived childbirth, she had to face the risk of her husband dying early, too.

Yet, through it all, moms have carried on, focusing on the welfare of their families.

Proverbs 31 classically illustrates modern, Christian women. They care for their families, have demanding work, and help those around them. No one goes without, even the less fortunate.

But can anyone "have it all?" Is "having it all" worth it? No.

Instead, we are simply called to do our best. Sometimes our best is a microwaved meal or opening a can. God wants us to focus on doing our best—not striving to have it all—here.

He has it all. Let Him help clean up the messes we've created today.

Peace and Prosperity

May the Lord *bless* you from Zion all the days of your life; may you see the prosperity of Jerusalem.

Psalm 128:5

We all want prosperity. We want our families, our finances, and our futures to prosper. Most people think that it's up to their efforts exclusively, or they depend on "luck" to bring about any improvements. Of course, they're wrong. Only God can make us prosperous. He'll use our efforts, but only in ways that accomplish His goals.

In the Old Testament, God chose to put His earthly "dwelling place" in Jerusalem, a gritty, complex, and confounding city. It's worth noting that Jerusalem was destroyed more than once because her people frequently abandoned Him, despite God wanting only to love and protect her.[19]

God has now decided to *bless* Jerusalem again in our lifetimes. And He'll *bless* us again, too, despite the ruin we've made of our lives.

Pray for Jerusalem's continued prosperity today, and ask Him to *bless* everyone else right along with it!

The Bigger the Better

Jabez cried out to the Lord, "Oh, that you would *bless* me and enlarge my territory!"

1 Chronicles 4:10

Bigger is always better, right? A bigger house, job, and bank account. Praying for these things may sound selfish, but Jabez wasn't shy about asking for more, and we shouldn't be, either.

The real question is: can we be wealthy *and* godly?

We know we're called to love God and each other, particularly the poor. Hidden in this command is the fact that wealth in the Bible is either a *blessing* or a curse. It's a *blessing* in the hands of the faithful: think of Abraham, Isaac, Jacob, Job, and Joseph of Arimathea, all of whom were rich, and all of whom were great lovers of God.

Yet possessions can be a curse if the primary purpose is accumulation without attention to the afflicted.

Praying for material blessings is fine; what we do with those *blessings* today is the measure of our character.

Milk and Honey

Look down from heaven, Your holy dwelling place, and *bless* Your people Israel, and the land You have given us as You promised on oath to our forefathers, a land flowing with milk and honey.

Deuteronomy 26:15

"Milk and honey" means health and happiness. Milk gives us strength, and honey makes life sweet. God promised those to His people because He loved them, not because of their goodness.

He loves us too, and our milk and honey doesn't necessarily consist of physical health or piece of land. Ours is a spiritual, and subtler, promise.

God uses our circumstances and our faith to help us enter the personal Promised Land He's crafted for us.

God provides all the milk we can drink so we can be strong, but He also provides the honey, so we are able to appreciate the sweetness of His promise.

God has provided our own personal Promised Land. Are we entering into it today?

In-laws and Outlaws

"The Lord *bless* him!" Naomi said to her daughter-in-law.

Ruth 2:20

Anybody who has ever been married knows about in-laws. While they can often be a troublesome bunch, they can also be a real *blessing*. Jesus even mentions in-law tensions when He was discussing why He came to Earth. In-laws can sometimes seem more like outlaws!

On the other hand, the book of Ruth illustrates the opposite: the love and care of a foreign daughter-in-law showed her mother-in-law she was better than seven sons.

We don't get to pick our family; God does. We may not always agree with His choices, yet we're called to love them (and try our best to like them!). They may not return our affection, but tit-for-tat relationships don't exist in God's world.

Unconditional love does and unconditional love is the most powerful force in the universe.[20]

Acquiring an in-law can feel like getting an organ transplant; it's painful but is ultimately designed to be life-giving.

Let's express our love to everyone today, especially to any and all in-laws.

Bending the Rules

Blessed are those who keep His statutes and seek Him with all their heart.

Psalm 119:2

Some people are strict law abiders, and others are law benders. Law abiders follow the rules, even when the rules seem unfair or too restrictive. Law benders understand the need for rules but often just keep the ones they like and ignore the ones they don't.

Bear in mind for a moment that Old Testament laws were written in stone; New Testament laws are written in our hearts.

Now notice that the second half of the verse shows God's intent.

He wants us to seek Him with the sincerity of our heart, not the letter of the law.

He wants us to *know* Him.

When we love someone, they don't have to write down what they "like;" we already know it. When we seek God, we don't get a written list from Him, either. When we spend time with Him, we'll quickly learn to know what He likes and doesn't like.

Getting to know Him better today is up to us, like it or not!

Evil Intent

Blessed is the one who does this, the person who holds it fast, who keeps the Sabbath without desecrating it, and keeps their hands from doing any evil.

Isaiah 56:2

Evil isn't something we dwell on today. We usually think it refers to terrorists, vicious murderers, or psychopaths like Hitler and his kind. We live in a world where any other reference to evil sounds either superstitious or unusually paranoid.

Yet, the Bible uses the word *evil* over 400 times.

We always like to think of ourselves as good. Very good even! But evil isn't just mean behavior; evil can also refer to deliberately selfish actions.

Simply stated, evil is sin...and we sin *all the time.*

In fact, we're incapable of *not* sinning.

Keeping our hands from evil is a great goal. When we are evil, and we know when we are, we get to repent, turn away from the evil, and ask for forgiveness. This is what Jesus died to give us.

When we say the Lord's Prayer, we ask God to "deliver us from evil." Pray He'll do that for us today.

Kid's Stuff

You will be *blessed* more than any other people; none of your men or women will be childless, nor will any of your livestock be without young.

Deuteronomy 7:14

In the Bible, children are always seen as a *blessing*, a sign of God's favor. Society in those days didn't have social security or retirement planning, so grown children were the key to survival later in life. Without children, old age simply meant poverty.

God didn't make the promise in this verse just to be nice. A few verses earlier, He conditioned His *blessing* on Israel's continued obedience to Him. Later, when they disobeyed, they suffered severely.

Today, many people have children, but many don't. It's often biology, but increasingly, it's also a choice that keeps a couple from having a child. These days, though, we don't have to worry about our future (whether we have children or not). Jesus came to take away any conditions on God's love.

We don't measure God's love by kids or cattle anymore. It's now, thankfully, unconditionally immeasurable, and it's called grace!

Thankfully, it's not some dense theological concept. It's kid's stuff. Jesus said we need to have the faith of a child.

Do we today?

Faint Praise

Though while they count themselves *blessed*—
and people praise you when you prosper—
they will join those who have gone before
them, who will never again see the light of
life. People that have wealth without understanding are like the beasts that perish.

Psalm 49:18-20

Praise can be a great motivator. Many studies have
looked at the effects of praise and found that we can't
deny its effects.

When praise is genuine, it makes men out of mice.
When it's false, it's a nicely wrapped lie.

We all share the same ultimate fate: death. What
happens next depends solely on our faith in Jesus and
His power to save us from death, the eternal kind.

Receiving sincere, well-deserved praise is wonderful, but ultimately, all of that will be forgotten. The only
thing God remembers is our relationship with His Son.

Spend more time praising Him, instead of ourselves
or others, today.

Shine On

May God be gracious to us and *bless* us and make His face shine upon us.

Psalm 67:1

The movie *The Shining* focused on the effects of isolation on a family confined in a snow-bound hotel. Mental illness overwhelms the husband and father, which leads to tragic results. There is something to be said for the movie's premise...

Isolation is almost always tragic. That is why solitary confinement is so dreaded.

We're created to be in community with others, whether we like them or not. Paul cautions spouses to limit even temporary separations from daily life because doing so can lead to temptation.[21]

We all like to be independent, but God's shining only happens when we're in a relationship with Him and others. We were never created to be alone, which is why God created Eve for Adam.

What relationship can we improve upon today?

Green with Envy

Long may he live. May gold from Sheba be given him. May people ever pray for him, and *bless* him all day long.

Psalm 72:15

We are all naturally envious, whether over someone's job, possessions, love life, looks, the list goes on and on. In fact, our envy is unlimited.

Israel envied other nations because they all had kings. God warned about transferring power to a human king, but they wanted one so badly, they begged God until He agreed. This verse is a prayer for the king's well-being. He symbolized the strength and health of the country.

We no longer have Earthly kings whose word means life or death. The One Great King we have now doesn't need to be prayed for; instead, we need to pray for His *blessings* upon us and to have *all* that He wants us to have.

Instead of looking enviously at anyone else today, look up to our great King. He is the Pearl of Great Price,[22] and He is not just all-powerful, He is Almighty!

APRIL 6

Last but Not Least

About Naphtali he said: "Naphtali is abound-
ing with the favor of the Lord and is full of His
blessing; he will inherit southward to the lake."

Deuteronomy 33:23

Naphtali was the "least" of Jacob's twelve sons; he is
almost always listed last. When the Israelites marched
through the desert, Naphtali marched in the very rear.
This means he and his tribe ate all the dust kicked up
by the eleven tribes in front of them: hundreds of thousands of people. Not an enviable position.

In this verse, we see God *blessing* them by giving
Naphtali the best portion of the Promised Land: the
shoreline of the Sea of Galilee.

It's so typical of God to save the best for last. Jesus
did that when He turned wine into water. He did it
again when He picked "nobody," fishermen, to carry
His message.

Then He picked nobodies like us to inherit eternal
life.

What can we do today for the other nobodies in our
life?

The Good, the Bad, and the Ugly

He *blessed* them and their numbers increased,
and He did not let their herds diminish.

Psalm 107:38

The Lord gives wonderful things to everyone: the good, the bad, and the ugly. It makes sense when we get our blessings because we think we're good and deserve them.

It's when the bad and the ugly are *blessed* that we get mad.

They don't deserve it, and they won't bother to thank God because they don't even believe in Him!

What gives?

In this verse, God's people are being blessed, but in the next verse, they'll be cursed. Whether any of it is fair doesn't matter; Jesus said the owner of the vineyard could do whatever he wished with his own money.

Let's not focus on what someone else got or didn't get.

Let's focus on being thankful for what He's done for us.

Showing God our thankfulness may be the only good thing we really do today.

Truth or Dare

Who ever invokes a *blessing* in the land will do
so by the God of truth.

Isaiah 65:16

When Pilate asked Jesus, "What is truth?" Jesus
didn't answer.

Many people silently ask that question daily. Whole
religions and philosophies have been developed to find
"truth." They probably wish Jesus had given Pilate a
quick and profound explanation, which could have
spared them all that effort!

But Jesus had already declared the answer to those
who are ready to hear: He is the Way, the Truth, and the
Life, and no one comes to God except through Him.[23]

By accepting this simple fact, we accept Him and everything He is.

Which is the real problem, isn't it? Accepting Jesus
means we must acknowledge we're sinners and need
forgiveness. Who likes that?

Most people don't like that truth and won't submit
to Him. They spend their lives in the endless pursuit of
"truths" that are, unfortunately, false.

We all know that the truth can sometimes be scary,
and we often don't want to hear it.

Do we really want to know the truth today?

Blame Game

Blessed are those whose ways are blameless,
who walk according to the law of the Lord.

Psalm 119:1

Nobody likes being blamed. Instead, we like to shift the responsibility onto other people. Even if we can't find a human scapegoat, we will try to deflect the focus to circumstances beyond our control.

Sometimes those excuses work, but usually, we have to pay the price for our own mistakes.

God gave Moses His laws; in fact, He gave him a detailed rulebook. The problem was nobody could keep from breaking God's law, so instead of asking God for help and grace, they invented interpretations to avoid the blame.

It didn't work, and all of those people died in their sin.

Yet, with His death on the cross, Jesus took the blame for all of our sins and all of our failures. We simply just have to acknowledge Him as Lord and Savior.

He knows the truth and wants us to accept responsibility for our sins and stop playing the blame game. Today.

You Are What You Eat

Bring me some game and prepare me some tasty food to eat, so that I may give you my *blessing* in the presence of the Lord before I die.

Genesis 27:7

We need food to live, and we tend to eat the same things repeatedly. If it's too much junk food, we become obese, and our health suffers. The bottom line is we sometimes don't eat what is good for us because we don't want to!

Isaac was ready to eat what he thought might be his last meal. He knew what he liked, and he knew who he wanted to cook it. Yet God had other plans for Isaac, and He does for us, too.

We spend too much time digesting junk because it's all around us. We get full with self-centeredness and sin.

Instead, God wants us to grow strong on the Bread of Life and digest His Scriptures.

We are what we eat. Are we really ready for a steady diet of the Bread of Life by reading the Bible today, or are we going to stick with the junk?

Free at Last

He also said, *"blessed* be the Lord, the God of Shem! May Canaan be the slave of Shem. May God extend the territory of Japheth; may Japheth live in the tents of Shem, and may Canaan be his slave."

Genesis 9:26-27

Bob Dylan once said, "You're gonna have to serve somebody," and he was right. We're slaves to our work, our family, our habits, and our sins. We're slaves when we don't have the liberty to refuse a command from the slave master.

And the most abusive masters are ourselves.

As Christians, we need to change. We're no longer slaves to ourselves; we're now accountable to God, our new Master. [24] According to Micah, that means we're to act justly, love mercy, and walk humbly before Him.[25] How simple—and hard—is that?

But think about the reward.

He promises to set us free today.

Pony Up

Supply them liberally from your flock and threshing floor, and your winepress. Give to them as the Lord your God has *blessed* you.

Deuteronomy 15:14

For some, giving may seem like a natural inclination. They may give to various causes: to correct wrongs, to build something for the future, or to help the helpless.

The total amount any of us gives away, however, is minuscule compared to our wealth, the wealth God gave us.

Generously, Jesus gave His life, and we're often reluctant to make gifts that aren't tax-deductible!

The Old Testament requires we give a tenth. While Jesus didn't specify a number or percentage in the New Testament, the early Church shared everything.[26] Imagine what good a fraction of that would do if we all did our part!

Is today the time to pony up for the good of the gospel, or are we going to wait until tomorrow, or the next day, or the next day?

Beat the Odds

> However, there need be no poor people
> among you, for in the land the Lord your God
> is giving you to possess as your inheritance,
> He will richly *bless* you.
>
> **Deuteronomy 15:4**

In utopia, everything is perfect: health, wealth, and pain-free lives. That's the picture that God gave the Israelites, and in order to receive it, they only had to believe in Him and follow His commandments. They would have no poor people because He would bless them.

All they had to do was obey Him.

They didn't, and neither do we.

Jesus said there will always be poor people.

They aren't the problem. Poor attitudes toward them are.

He also said very few rich people get into Heaven. That's because they don't sense a need for Him; instead, they think they have everything.

According to the statistics, we are the richest people in the history of the world. Let's try to beat the odds of rich people getting into Heaven by blessing those with less today.

Insult to Injury

Blessed are you when people hate you, when they exclude you and insult you and reject you as evil, because of the Son of Man.

Luke 6:22

Being hated, insulted, or excluded is very hurtful. We're social by nature, which is why we live near other people. We need social interaction. It's painful when we've tried to be nice and connect with co-workers, family members, or so-called friends, but in return, they don't seem to want anything to do with us.

It is especially hurtful when this rejection stems from our Christian faith.

In this verse, Jesus is telling us to be ready for all of this, and later in the Bible, Peter says not to be surprised at the trials we will experience; instead, we should *rejoice* in knowing we suffer for Christ.

Insults and injuries are hard to endure, but He endured far worse. As someone once said, "Don't pray for an easy life; pray to be a strong person."

Pray for strength today.

Thirst Quencher

Blessed are those who hunger and thirst for
righteousness, for they will be filled.

Matthew 5:6

Being hungry and thirsty can sometimes be symp-
toms of malnourishment. We can go many days without eating, but very few without drinking. Once we've
eaten and had enough to drink, we're full.

It's the same with our relationship with God.

There's something in the human soul that longs to be
spiritually fed, to drink from the fountain of life. Righteousness is what God wants us to experience. It can
be defined as being "right with God." In other words,
righteousness is to be accepted by Him as a son or a
daughter.

In this verse, Jesus is promising that our prayers to
be more like God will be answered. He is saying that
if we desire it, we'll be "right" with Him. We'll be filled
with His righteousness.

How hungry and thirsty are we for righteousness
today?

Court Side

Blessed are those You choose and bring near to live in Your courts.

Psalm 65:4

We love to be close to the action. Courtside seats at basketball games and fifty-yard line tickets to football games are the most treasured. They are also the most expensive, for obvious reasons. Sitting up front makes for a much better experience than being in the nosebleed sections.

Closeness to God works that way, too. We clearly see Him working and feel His presence, yet we can't buy the "seats" the psalmist is speaking of. God gives them away to those of us who *really* want to be part of the game plan He's mapped out.

Plus, we won't be receiving any individual recognition; all of that goes to Him. We have to humble ourselves and faithfully follow the Great Coach's instructions.

But these seats in God's courts are worth far more than the price we pay, however, because not only are they worth the price of admission, they have a guaranteed return on investment.

Are we willing to pay what it takes to sit in His courts today?

Town and Country

You will be *blessed* in the city.

Deuteronomy 28:3

Urbanization has taken over the world. Everywhere, scores of people move from rural areas to cities daily. Usually, they go to the city looking for a better life.

Better lives, however, can be measured in different ways. We all want to improve our family's economics, education, and opportunities. There is nothing wrong with that.

Often, though, that quest for a better life comes at the expense of a *simpler* life, and our sense of community can fall by the wayside, as well.

God has promised to bless us wherever we go when we seek His kingdom first.

Let's make sure our relationship with God is first, and we'll always be blessed, wherever we are, today.

Wake Up

Blessed are the people of whom this is true;
blessed are the people whose God is the Lord.

Psalm 144:15

It seems that truth now means "what we want to believe." What we do is okay as long as it doesn't hurt anybody else, right? This is supposed to make us more free, but truthfully, that type of freedom is a myth.

In modern terms, we can often substitute the word "freedom" for "self-centered."

Someone once said truth is truth regardless of the source. We know God is the source, and Jesus is the truth and the light.

We need to speak the truth in love and turn on the Light of the world, so everyone we connect with today will wake up and see Him through us.

APRIL 19

What's the Rush?

Abraham was now old and well advanced in
years and the Lord *blessed* him in every way.

Genesis 24:1

We all want to grow old gracefully. Some people
say they don't want to get too old and fall apart. Others
want to live as long as possible. They ask, "What's the
rush?"

Many people want the quality of their life to determine when they are "ready to go." The Bible would ar-
gue that it's up to God to set the quantity of our lives,
not just the quality.

In this verse, Abraham was probably 140 years old
when God spoke to him. He died at 175, which means
that he still had thirty-five years left of life.

How much time do we have left? God has measured
our days and expects us to use each one well.

God is not in a rush, but He does expect results.

Are we going to focus today on God's results or our
own?

Multiplication

When I saw him he was only one man, and I
blessed him and made him many.

Isaiah 51:2

God loves multiplying. Jesus multiplied the loaves
and fishes; Elijah multiplied oil and flour. In Genesis 1,
everything multiplies.

Yet the world has clear winners and losers. Some
things don't multiply; they die out.

This verse is about Abraham, who miraculously had
Isaac at the age of 100 years old (Sarah, his wife, was
ninety). God then *multiplied* Isaac into two different
people groups, one of which being the Jewish people,
who still endure.

God likes taking very tiny things and making them
grand. He does it to make us understand that what we
think is small, weak, old, or worn is often the material
He really likes to work with. This should give us hope as
we grow smaller, weaker, older, and wear out.

He is still molding us into something even greater.

Will we let Him do that today?

Payback

Have You not put a hedge around him and his household and everything he has? You have *blessed* the work of his hands, so that his flocks and herds are spread throughout the land.

Job 1:10

We all like to think that if we do good, we'll be *blessed.* Sounds like karma, right? Don't we expect to be paid back for all the "good things" we've been doing? The "prosperity gospel" movement tends to say that we deserve nice things because we're such nice people. God owes us; we want a payback for our efforts!

Job found out that God has His own priorities. God rewards our efforts, but not necessarily with physical *blessings.* We are called to be obedient, period. Jesus says we should act like slaves who work all day and serve their master's dinner, only getting a break when everything has been done. That's not how we would have designed the system. Our reward may be on this side of Heaven or that. We have to wait, just like Job.

Can we wait patiently for God today, or are we expecting an immediate payback?

If Only

The *blessing* if you obey the commands of the Lord your God that I am giving you today.

Deuteronomy 11:27

We love to "if only" ourselves.

"If only we had said this."

"If only we had said that."

"If only we had done this differently!"

We are constantly second-guessing ourselves about what other people think of us. Someone once said, "Don't worry what people think about you because they don't think about you very often." This is true, true, true.

God, on the other hand, is always thinking about us. He has an amazing plan to *bless* our lives if only we keep His commands. Yet He doesn't force them on us. He gives us the free will to obey or not.

Amazingly, He *blesses* us even when we fail.

How much more would He bless us if only we were more obedient today?

Be Nice

...and all peoples on earth will be blessed through you.

Genesis 12:3

We all try to be nice: we're nice when we allow a car to move in front of us during traffic, we're nice to the waitress and store clerk, we're nice to policemen. Ultimately, we're often nicer to strangers than the people who are closest to us. This can be because we take our loved ones for granted or because they have failed to live up to our expectations of them. The phrase "familiarity breeds contempt" can be all too true.

More likely, we've failed to live up to the expectations for ourselves, and we need an outlet for those frustrations.

God is incredibly generous. Not only does He *bless* us, but He *blesses* those we *bless*.

Let's start blessing those we live and work with (and ourselves, too).

God is blessing us right now. Go and do likewise today.

Hearing Test

The Lord will open the heavens, the storehouse of His bounty, to send rain on your land in season and to *bless* all the work of your hands.

Deuteronomy 28:12

We must believe God wants to bless us. Like any good father, He loves us and wants the best for us; after all, we're His children.

Kids come in three sizes: little, middle & big.

Parenting little kids takes the energy, but they tend to want to obey. Middle kids (or teenagers) question and sometimes rebel but can usually be controlled by withholding privileges. Big, or adult, kids are autonomous; they can be reasoned with and sometimes persuaded, but they are in total control.

We're all God's adult kids. We don't have to listen to anything He says, and we often ignore Him. Yet listening to God is a really good idea. Mark Twain once remarked about how smart his "old man" got after he turned twenty-one.

God is our Father. Let's listen up and obey Him so He will pour His blessings out upon us today.

APRIL 25

Second Chance

As for Ishmael, I have heard you: I will surely
bless him; I will make him fruitful and greatly
increase his numbers.

Genesis 17:20

Everybody likes to win, and everybody likes a winner. We rarely remember who got second place; however, we all come in second, third, or even last place all
the time.

If we're honest, we lose more than we win.

If a baseball player hits .300, they're famous, despite
the fact that they did not get a hit seventy percent of the
time. This is much how God works. He is interested in
the end result, not just the process.

He is the God of second chances.

God was kind to Ishmael. He was Abraham's firstborn son and Isaac's older half-brother, but he was not
chosen by God to be Abraham's heir. He came in second. But God gave him twelve sons whose descendants
became modern-day Arabs, who are a huge population
group today.

Not bad for second place.

God continually bails us out and saves us, even when
we deserve to be called out. Remember to thank God for
all the second chances He will give us today.

Star Struck

I will surely *bless* you and make your descendants as numerous as the stars in the sky and as the sand on the seashore.

Genesis 22:17

Stars are awe-inspiring. In the city, they're like little flashlights, blinking through the night haze. In the country, they're astounding: uncountable, brilliant pinpricks against the black of space. Ancient people worshiped stars as gods. Astrologers still insist that they control our lives.

God often uses stars as examples of His generosity, His *blessings*.

While Abraham was nobody special, he had faith, so God made him into someone great. He told Abraham that He would make his descendants as numerous as the stars in the sky. Jesus said if we even have faith as small as a mustard seed, we can move mountains.

We all want to be stars, at least in the eyes of people who matter. Let's start by practicing our faith and using the measure of it that we've been given.

That is sure to brighten up everyone around us today!

Walk Don't Run

For I command you today to love the Lord your God, to walk in His ways, and to keep His commands, decrees and laws; then you will live and increase, and the Lord your God will *bless* you in the land you are entering to possess.

Deuteronomy 30:16

Strolling means to walk in a relaxed and unstressed way. We don't do much of that now. Whether we're late for a meeting, don't want to get somewhere last, or even just don't want to miss our favorite show, we're always in a hurry.

We're literally on the run, and we are out of breath.

Yet God's never in a hurry. He's not slow or fast; He's always on time.

Our life with God should be a walk. Jesus never used "run" in a positive manner. Even when the writer of Hebrews said to run our race with patience,[27] he meant in a measured way, the way marathon runners do.

We're called to *walk* toward and with God. Then we'll have time for a relaxed, personal conversation and really get to know Him.

Walk with God, and don't try to run from Him today; you won't get very far anyway!

Tough Stuff

David asked the Gibeonites, "What shall I do for you? How shall I make amends so that you will *bless* the Lord's inheritance?"

2 Samuel 21:3

Not all *blessings* are bound to be good for everybody. In this verse, David is asking the Gibeonites how he could help to remove a drought. Interestingly enough, the drought was caused by crimes committed by the late King Saul.

The answer from the Gibeonites was not a blessing to seven of Saul's descendants. The Gibeonites asked for permission to put these seven people to death. More interesting is that David granted their request. Most interesting still is that God then provided rain, a blessing. This is tough stuff!

We often don't know why things happen; God sometimes lets the wicked harm the righteous. Job, Jeremiah, and Habakkuk asked why, and they all received the same answer: *"Wait."*

God's sense of justice isn't limited by time. We always want justice right now, but praying for justice is risky because everyone's sins deserve severe punishment. Even though God might avenge you in a way that suits His purposes, the apostle Paul told us to do good to our enemies.[28] That's tough stuff, too.

So don't demand justice. Instead, pray for mercy. Hopefully, God will give it to us today.

Bad Guys

He loved to pronounce a curse—may it come
upon him; he found no pleasure in *blessing*—
may it be far from him.

Psalm 109:17

There's no shortage of bad people. There has never
been. We live in times where news of scandals and
crimes are flashed before us every minute, so it's easy
to think the entire world has lost its balance.

It hasn't.

Radio personality Paul Harvey said, "In times like
these, it's nice to remember that there have always been
times like these."

God doesn't change either. He's not surprised by any
of the current antics and crises, nor should we be. Ultimately, He will have the last word.

Jesus told us not to worry and to have faith that He
knows what He's doing.[29] While that may be more faith
than we can sometimes muster, let's use what we have
and pray for the peace that passes all understanding.

One thing is certain: we will need that today.

Fill in the Blanks

When Samuel reached him, Saul said, "The Lord *bless* you! I have carried out the Lord's instructions."

1 Samuel 15:13

God is seen by some as distant and disinterested. They believe that He gives general guidelines, and the rest is up to us to "fill in the blanks." Many people think God is either too busy to focus on our problems, or He simply doesn't care.

In a previous verse, Samuel gave Saul specific orders, but Saul decided to interpret those to his own advantage. Then, to make matters worse, he lied about it.

Bad idea. Samuel quickly told Saul that his kingdom was being taken away from him because of his disobedience.

Jesus said God knows the number of hairs on our head. He wants us to know Him better and become more like Him. Just like Samuel did for Saul, He has given us precise instructions, but we often only follow the ones we like.

If we let God fill in the blanks for us, we won't have any empty spaces.

Instead, He'll give us the complete sentences, paragraphs, chapters, and, ultimately, the book He wants to write for our lives.

Let Him start letting Him fill in the blanks in our lives today.

Rate of Return

He will love you and *bless* you, and increase
your numbers.

Deuteronomy 7:13

The national American pastime seems to be planning for retirement. We want to maximize our rate of return, and we never want to run out of money or be dependent on anyone. We cherish our independence. Unfortunately, we can't control the stock market, real estate prices, or even our health.

Ultimately, we have to admit we have no control.

God has total control over the big and small pictures of our lives. He's not worried about our rate of return or the amount of our home equity. He's interested in our relationship with Him and other people.

God pays great dividends, but we have to be totally invested.

Invest everything with Him today.

MAY 2

The Reigning Champion

May his name endure forever; may it continue as long as the sun. All nations will be *blessed* through him. [...] and they will call him *blessed*.

Psalm 72:17

Endurance is easy to talk about, but we really don't want to endure pain, suffering, or even annoyances; in all actuality, we just want all of those to *stop*. While we admire athletes, statesmen, and heroes who faced trials, few of us would volunteer to go through what it took to accomplish their feats.

In this verse, King Solomon is praying for a successful reign in order to bless *the people* of Israel. God answered his prayer (and then some) because his motives were right.

In the same way, God gives us endurance if we have a lasting goal: Heaven. Knowing there is a reward for our challenges gives us the courage and strength to overcome our insecurities and problems.

We need to pray for ourselves and other Christians to have the staying power and commitment to encourage others. In this way, our short "reign" here will be successful, too.

With Jesus's help, we can win the fights we will face today.

Dead Wrong

Your descendants will take possession of the cities of their enemies, and through your offspring all nations on earth will be *blessed*, because you obeyed me.

Genesis 22:17-18

The phrase "possession is nine-tenths of the law" is mostly true, but possessing something may mean we've had to fight for it. Once we have control, someone else has to try to take it away, which is not always easy.

Whatever we possess belongs to us until someone proves they're stronger than us, or some authority tells us to give it up.

In this verse, God promised Abraham that his descendants would prosper, materially and spiritually. The apostle Paul says we are those descendants.[30]

Without question, God has *blessed* us materially, but it's the spiritual *blessing* we'll enjoy for eternity. The saying "you can't take it with you" is dead wrong. We can't take stuff, but we can possess eternal life forever.

What would we leave behind, and what would we take with us if we died today?

Mamma Mia

I will *bless* her and will surely give you a son
by her.

Genesis 17:16

Sarah is the most fascinating woman in the Old Testament. While she is an obedient wife and mother, she
is also jealous, spiteful, and realistic. When God says
she'll become pregnant at ninety years old, who could
blame her for laughing (and then lying about that)?

This miracle made her famous because, despite
being thoroughly imperfect, she loved God and her
husband.

God never selects "perfect" people to do His will because they'll think it was their innate goodness that
caused the *blessing*. God likes screw-ups as heroes and
the severely flawed as heroines so the glory focuses on
Him, not us.

Sarah is our role model who shows us that people
with major imperfections are saved despite their flaws
and sins.

If God can use a jealous, spiteful ninety-year-old to
accomplish His will, what can He do with us today?

Mystery Man

Then Melchizedek king of Salem brought out
bread and wine. He was priest of God Most
High, and he blessed Abram, saying, *"Blessed
be Abram by God Most High, Creator of heav-
en and earth."*

Genesis 14:18-19

In this verse, we see the mystery man of the Bible,
Melchizedek. He appears out of nowhere, but he's immediately respected, he helps Abram, and then, as
quickly as he appeared, he disappears into history.

He's like those people we immediately and deeply
connect with, and then, poof, they're gone. We've all
experienced this with someone: maybe they sat next
to us on a flight or at a restaurant. They give us advice
because they're not entangled in our lives; they're like
angels sent to pinpoint the solution.

God will give us answers, but He often uses others
because He knows that we don't always want to listen
to Him directly. We do need to be careful who we listen
to, though, since not everyone's Melchizedek.

Life can seem very mysterious, so let's start looking
for the Melchizedeks the Lord may bring into our lives
today.

Triple Play

The Lord Almighty will bless them, saying, *"Blessed* be Egypt My people, Assyria My
handiwork, and Israel My inheritance."
Isaiah 19:25

Have you ever thought God can seem *too* generous?
This looks like a triple play because He's *blessing* all three
countries. Now we know that He gives good things to
people (and countries) who are His (and our) enemies,
yet that can seem so unfair when we are sometimes
struggling just to pay the bills, keep our jobs, and hold
our family together.

Why is He *blessing* them? They don't even care about
Him, they may even hate Him.

While we would never say God is wrong, in our
hearts, we can't help but wonder if He is sometimes
misguided.

In this verse, He's *blessing* Egypt *and* Assyria. At the
time this was written, Egypt was Israel's on-again, off-
again ally, and former slave master. Assyria had outright invaded Israel and carried away half the people.

Regardless, God is *blessing* them.

We don't know what will happen tomorrow, but God
does. That's why Jesus said, "Love your enemies."

And He didn't say start tomorrow; He wants us to
start today.

Comfort Food

> When you have crossed the Jordan, these tribes shall stand on Mount Gerizem to *bless* the people: Simeon, Levi, Judah, Issachar, Joseph and Benjamin.
>
> **Deuteronomy 27:12**

There's nothing like relaxing after a hard day. You change clothes, watch a bit of TV, eat a nice dinner, maybe have a drink. This all helps the stress of a tough day fade away.

Comfort food means exactly what it says: its taste and smell help to comfort and unwind us.

The Israelites were ready to get more comfortable after forty years of walking, sleeping, and eating in the desert. Their children knew nothing else. God wanted to *bless* the Israelites, and in the same way, He wants to *bless* and comfort us, too.

But let's not get too comfortable. There are many people suffering and in pain. A saying attributed to Mr. Dooley, a fictional Chicago bartender created by Finley Peter Dunne, is that we should comfort the afflicted and afflict the comfortable.

That sounds like a recipe for fun today, doesn't it?

Basket Case

Your basket and your kneading trough will be
blessed.

Deuteronomy 28:5

We like order. We put our socks, shoes, and under-
wear in specific places so we can find them in a hurry.
We organize our work to make it flow smoothly and ef-
fectively. Baskets are sometimes still used to efficiently
move bulky items and to keep things separated.

God knows we need order, and He promises to bless
our baskets. Whether it's our health, wealth, or worries,
He carries the heavy stuff and keeps things from spill-
ing from one aspect of our lives into another.

So often, we tend to believe our problems are huge
and unsolvable. God knows, however, that countless
others have faced the same issues and not only survived
but thrived.

God will bless our baskets today, and He will make
sure that nothing falls through the cracks.

MAY 9

Rich and Famous

The *blessing* of the Lord brings wealth, and He
adds nothing to it.

Proverbs 10:22

We have an interesting relationship with money.
Most of us secretly like to be rich, and while we often
resent the success of another, we still pray for more.

In the Bible, riches are usually seen as God's *blessing*, but the love of money is condemned. Wealth isn't
just about money. The Beatles wrote that money "can't
buy me love," and they were right. While money can be
used to help people, it can never buy what's important:
love. Wealth can be used to help people and make us
comfortable, but it can also be corrosive and make us
controlling.

Almost always, more money seems to equal less dependence on God.

It's okay to pray for wisdom, wealth, and health, but
most of all, pray for humility because once we're truly
humble, we can be trusted with real wealth.

Remember that God knows what we need to get
through today, and more money will almost never play
a part in it.

High Life

As soon as you enter the town, you will find him before he goes to the high place to eat. The people will not begin eating until he comes, because he must *bless* the sacrifice.

1 Samuel 9:13

High places are a big part of our culture. We envy people who inhabit the top floor or executive suite. "Climb the ladder of success" is our mantra. Esteemed professionals are "top drawer."

Although it was forbidden, Israel sometimes offered sacrifices to God at a "high place" because, as their thinking went, the higher in elevation you got, the closer to God you must be.

Jesus turned that thinking on its head. He told us to serve the poor, the people in the ditch, the lowest rung of society's ladder. Jesus asks us to put ourselves on their level, following His example.

If we want to experience His high life today, we'll need to get down on our knees and see where He leads us.

Just Right

Blessed are those who act justly, who always
do what is right.

Psalm 106:3

If everyone who always did the right thing were
lined up in a single file, it would be a very short line. In
fact, Jesus would be the only One in line![31]

It's not always easy knowing exactly what is right
because what one person thinks is right, another may
think is wrong. Society's different views on the death
penalty and immigration are good examples of this.

Acting justly can be as challenging when deciding
who's right and who's wrong. We know this because
fitting the punishment to the crime is a subject of great
debate.

To accomplish justice, though, what God really
wants us to do is listen to people and love them. A proverb sometimes attributed to Mother Teresa says, "We're
not called to love the whole world, just one another."

If we show forgiveness and love, we can trust God to
take care of everything else.

Let's start today by doing what is right and just to
those closest to us.

No Limits

Where there is no revelation, people cast off restraint; but *blessed* is the one who heeds wisdom's instruction.

Proverbs 29:18

None of us likes being restrained. We all like our personal freedom, but sometimes restraint is needed for our own good. For instance, the threat of jail curbs drunk driving, and hospitals occasionally bind patients to their beds to keep them from harming themselves.

God's intention is not to restrain us but rather to guide us. He reveals what's best for us, then gives us the freedom to follow those directions.

Or to choose not to.

If we do follow those directions, we'll get wisdom, hope, and peace. The consequences of ignoring God are evident all around us because casting off restraint is self-destructive.

No-limits living can lead to a very frustrating life. While it may seem crazy, accepting God's boundaries will set us wonderfully free!

Do we want freedom or frustration today?

Random Acts of Kindness

Ammiel the sixth, Isaachar the seventh, and Peulentrai the eighth (For God had *blessed* Obed-Edom.)

1 Chronicles 26:5

God frequently blesses us in ways we don't expect; sometimes, He blesses us with things we never even requested! Obed-Edom experienced a classic example of God's unexpected blessings. Not only did God bless him with eight strong sons in a time when sons provided status, but his home was picked to house the Ark of the Covenant for three months.

Having the Ark of the Covenant in his home brought even more blessings, not just for him but his entire household.[32]

We've all been *blessed* by God's seemingly random acts of kindness.

But these acts aren't random. They are very deliberate acts of His kindness.

Remember to thank Him deliberately for the not-so-random acts of kindness He will provide to us today.

Forever and Ever

Now You have been pleased to *bless* the house
of Your servant, that it may continue forever
in your sight...

1 Chronicles 17:27

Forever is a long time; it's infinite! People visit astrologers and fortune-tellers in the hope of getting some control over their future, but the latter will only tell us what we want to hear.

We can plan and guess what the future holds, but God is the only One who knows what will happen today, tomorrow, and the days after.

In this verse, God promises David and his heirs a secure future; they'll be kings of Israel forever if they obey God's laws and honor Him alone.

They all failed, except for One: Jesus.

He's the One that holds our future, and if we believe and obey, our future in Heaven is safe with Him.

We will spend forever and ever in one of two places: Heaven or Hell. He lets us choose which one today.

Concerned Citizen

Saul replied, "The Lord *bless* you for your concern for me."

1 Samuel 23:21

Most of us are concerned about many of the same things in life, such as our finances, family frustrations, and health. Some people *declare* their concern is for others and not themselves, but the reply in Missouri would be "show me." In Texas, they might be accused of being "all hat and no cattle."

This verse shows an example of self-centered concern. It was well known that King Saul was hunting David to kill him. Faking concern for himself and his kingdom, Saul learnt David's location from men who were really only looking to gain his favor.

Don't we show the same false concern when we gossip? Christians especially love to say things like, "Oh pray for him...he's struggling," or "I'm concerned about her and need to share this burden." Then they gossip.

This is usually to make themselves look good while making others look bad, but God takes gossip very seriously. In Scripture, Paul ranks gossip with murder and blasphemy.[33]

If we are truly concerned for others, we have to ask Jesus for help with this; we usually don't, though, because we enjoy gossiping too much!

Is the source of your concern for others today rooted in goodness or gossip?

MAY 16

Sisterhood

And they *blessed* Rebekah and said to her,
"Our sister, may you increase to thousands
and thousands; may your offspring possess
the gates of their enemies."
Genesis 24:60

While many societies idealize sons, daughters are
often the overlooked force in the family. Boys are encouraged to go outward from home and venture into
the larger world, and while culture is changing, girls
have traditionally been taught to focus inward and tend
to the family's domestic needs.

In this verse, Rebekah is being blessed for her extraordinary faith and obedience to God. By leaving her
family on one day's notice to follow a stranger into a
foreign country and marry an unknown man, Rebekah broke a longstanding and deep-seated cultural
tradition.

How greatly was she *blessed* for her remarkable obedience? She became the mother of Jacob (later called
Israel)!

God's *blessings* await us, too, *if* we leave our emotionally and physically safe place.

Who knows what great adventure God has in store if
we will faithfully follow Him?

What comfort zone could He be calling us out of
today?

House and Home

Blessed are those who dwell in Your house;
they are ever praising You.

Psalm 84:4

Houses are not always homes, and a home isn't always a house. Home is more of a sanctuary: it can be a house, an apartment, a dorm room, or an RV. "Home" can even be a memory. Many people who move frequently refer to the place they grew up as their home, even if they haven't been back there in years. A house, on the other hand, may just be four walls and a roof; it is not permanent.

Although the temple was called God's house, He's never actually lived in any physical place. He lives everywhere, but what He would like to do is to make His home in our hearts so that He can be a part of our everyday lives. He wants to be there when we wake up and when we go to sleep. He wants our home to be His home, too.

Do we want Him to move in today, or would we rather just have Him pass through, clean things up a bit, and keep going so that He doesn't mess things up too much?

Are we a house or a home for God?

Command Performance

Praise the Lord. *Blessed* are those who fear the
Lord, who find delight in His commands.

Psalm 112:1

Most of us don't like being told what to do, so following orders isn't always easy. At work, we may be commanded to do things we don't feel like doing, just as the
law of our country may command us to follow rules we
don't agree with.

Many people seem to think that Christianity con-
sists of hundreds, if not thousands, of dos and don'ts.
Surprisingly, Jesus only gave us two commands.

First, we have to love God with all our heart and
mind; it takes plenty of faith to love an almighty yet
invisible God. We do this by following Him through
Scripture, prayer, and doing the works He asked to do.

The second command Jesus gave us is much harder: we must love other people as much as we love ourselves. That means putting others before ourselves, and
it takes supernatural strength to do that.

How are we going to obey both of those commands
today?

Face Down

Joab fell with his face to the ground to pay
him honor, and he *blessed* the king.

2 Samuel 14:22

Feelings of stage fright are very common. Giving a
presentation in front of an audience is said to be one of
the most stressful things a person can experience. Just
like Joab's meeting with King David in the verse above,
we also sometimes get the jitters when we meet someone famous.

But for those who believe, Jesus's death on the cross
removes our fear of meeting God. Without the cross,
we would not be worthy of staying in God's presence,
even for a moment, because we're sinners. Now, even
though we still sin, we can approach our Father in the
way Joab did before King David because Jesus bore our
punishment.

We can now approach God with our heads bowed
in honor and respect and no longer in shame and disgrace. We can look up, not down, today.

Shame on You

They may curse, but You will *bless*; when they attack they will be put to shame, but Your servant will rejoice.

Psalm 109:28

Shame is like a stain; it's a mark on someone's reputation. These days, even though many things that used to be shameful are accepted as normal—or, worse, even honored—curses and attacks can still shame people into submission. These attacks often use labels like "bigot," "hypocrite," "fanatic," and "sell-out."

God wants us to ignore all of this and focus our attention on Him.

He wants us to trust Him to protect us, provide for us, and give us everything we need to prosper. We may be cursed for being Christians, but we must still behave like Christians: we must love, forgive and trust in Jesus.

Shame only sticks if we do something wrong and don't repent. We've all acted shamefully at some time, but Jesus has already taken the hit for us, so we don't need to feel shame any longer.

All we're commanded to do today is bless our attackers, trust God, and rejoice!

In Harm's Way

> The Angel who has delivered me from all harm—may He *bless* these boys.
>
> **Genesis 48:16**

For a grandparent to *bless* a grandchild is a joyful thing. Being a grandparent is a great privilege and an equally great responsibility. Grandparents are expected to spoil their grandchildren! They also play the role of an advisor in a way parents often can't.

In this verse, Jacob thanked God for the opportunity to see his grandsons when he thought he would never even see them or his son, Joseph, again. Jacob worshiped God for delivering his beloved son and grandsons from harm.

The Bible tells us that through his life, Jacob found himself in harm's way many times, just as we have. He suffered and cried, just as we have. Yet God delivered him, in the sense that He didn't let Jacob's stupid and dishonest actions direct the course of his life.

God had mercy on Him and his descendants. He does the same for us.

Today, thank Him for His mercy and for the grandparents He gave us.

Finish Line

After David had finished sacrificing the burnt
offerings and fellowship offerings, he *blessed*
the people in the name of the Lord.

1 Chronicles 16:2

There's always a difference in the way we feel at
the start of a project and when it's finished. The start
is usually filled with optimism, while sometimes we're
disappointed in the finish.

Human life is the same way.

Everybody loves babies. They've yet to hurt anyone's feelings or cause harm. Teenagers are sometimes
moody and argumentative. Adults can be disagreeable
and unpleasant. Old people can be burdensome and,
occasionally, difficult.

Yet, God is involved with us from start to finish. He
wants us to run the race of life well and never get lazy
or lose our way. Some of us have had a bad start; let's
forget that and focus on running our race well.

Focus on the finish line.

Today, remember: He's waiting for us there, cheer-
ing us on.

Jackpot

The priests and the Levites stood to *bless* the people, and God heard them, for their prayer reached heaven, His holy dwelling place.

2 Chronicles 30:27

Prayer can be a powerful tool, but it can also be a source of frustration. Christ said He'll ask the Father to answer the prayers of His followers, but most people pray only when they really need help. The attitude is to sort of cross one's fingers and say, "I hope this works" instead of "Please Father, you promised this in Your Word…"

Still, Jesus never discouraged anyone from praying.

When we pray, sometimes the answer is "yes," but sometimes it's "no," and that can be the discouraging part.

Often it's "wait."

Although we wish it were so, God is not a slot machine who awards us jackpots. He's our Father. He knows what we need, when we need it, and the best way for us to receive it.

Having faith and patience is winning the true jackpot. Pray for that jackpot today.

Heart-Healthy

Blessed are those whose strength is in you,
whose hearts are set on pilgrimage.

Psalm 84:5

We love holidays and vacations because we don't have to work, but even those can quickly get overscheduled.

A long weekend away, or a vacation, helps accomplish the original intent of rest: revitalization of our bodies and spirits. Being away from routine can clear our heads.

Our minds can end up like many garages do, filled with disconnected stuff. Taking time away from dealing with that stuff helps us organize our thoughts and rediscover something valuable about ourselves. It also helps us clear out the junk.

Pilgrimage could be thought of as the vacation of the earlier centuries. Pilgrims took a long road trip to worship God.

We should, too, at least in our minds.

God wants us to rediscover Him while we take the time to rest in Him.

Start looking for a way to make that a priority. After all, we could use the break, especially today!

Mixed-Up

He sent messengers to the men of Jabesh Giliad to say to them, "The Lord *bless* you for showing kindness to Saul your master by burying him."

2 Samuel 2:5

Jabesh Gilead is a town with a mixed-up biblical history. First, it was destroyed by the Israelites for not contributing men to a battle. The town is later mentioned when it was attacked by another country, barely managed to hang on, and was eventually rescued by King Saul. In this verse, it's being praised for burying Saul's mutilated body.

The bottom line is they sinned, were later rescued and returned the favor.

Then David *blesses* them.

It's an example for us. We all sin and pay the penalty, sometimes serious ones. We're often mixed-up and under attack, and God rescues us again and again. When we're rescued, we can help rescue others who have been set back by their sins too.

Then we'll be *blessed* just like those in Jabesh Gilead.

Today try focusing on spiritual successes, not spiritual mistakes.

Brotherly Love

About Asher he said: "Most *blessed* is Asher; let him be favored by his brothers, and let him bathe his feet in oil."

Deuteronomy 33:24

Sibling rivalries are as old as Cain and Abel, whose issues ended in death and a curse. It's not uncommon for brothers and sisters to fight over inheritances, they might even be settling a score that started in the sandbox. Sadly, it's often easier to like a recent acquaintance more than a sibling we've known since birth.

In this verse, we see Moses *blessing* the tribe of Asher, the descendants of Jacob's twelve sons, and one of the twelve tribes of Israel. Asher wasn't among the leaders. In fact, here, the tribe is listed twelfth.

Yet Moses gives them a *blessing* of honor.

Asher is given that *blessing* because the lowly position made the tribe humble. Humility, not arrogance, is what God cherishes most in us. It is also what we treasure in others.

If we're humble toward everyone today, brotherly and sisterly love won't just be a slogan, it will be real!

Over Easy

But I would not listen to Balaam, so he *blessed* you again and again, and I delivered you out of his hand.

Joshua 24:10

We tend to think much of our life is set in stone and that either our family situations or past decisions have made our lives mostly unchangeable. This predictably can lead to frustration, anger, and depression. We feel stuck and believe there is nothing that can be done about it.

God doesn't see it that way.

He has a plan for our lives that doesn't depend on anything we've screwed up or the family challenges we have.

In this verse, the Lord took Balaam's curses and turned them into *blessings* for Israel, again and again! He'll do that for us. We just need to seek Him, listen to Him, and hope in Him.

We face challenges daily. If we trust Him, He'll guide, deliver and *bless* us over and over again, too!

Are we going to feel stuck or empowered today?

Tomorrowland

The Lord will send a blessing on your barns
and on everything you put your hand to. The
Lord will *bless* you in the land He is giving you.

Deuteronomy 28:8

Clouds of worry can overcome all of us. Sometimes they're wispy; other times, they're dark and frightening. We don't like to worry, and usually, we try to fight it and pray for relief.

The truth is, we're anxious because we don't trust God.

We want it fixed *now*, not in the hazy future. If He won't do it, then, by God, we'll try to do it ourselves.

That's never a good idea.

Despite what this verse says, we still worry. People in Jesus's time did too. But Jesus said to seek His kingdom first, not clothes, wealth, health, or anything else. He said to focus on today's challenges, not tomorrow's.

When we focus on seeking His kingdom today, He guarantees He will take care of tomorrow.

Big and Little

The Lord remembers us and will bless us; He
will bless His people Israel, He will bless the
house of Aaron, He will bless those who fear
the Lord—small and great alike.

Psalm 115:12-13

We all like to be remembered. We want to be remembered at Christmas and on our birthdays. We especially want to be remembered when we die. If possible, we all want to live on in the memories of our family and friends forever.

In this verse, God promises to *bless* all who acknowledge and fear Him—big and little.

Thankfully, we don't have to be supermen and superwomen.

It is good to remember, however, that God doesn't bless everyone. He only promises to *bless* those who *fear* Him, small and great alike. That takes us back to the humility lesson.

Those who don't fear Him don't need Him. He rightly reserves His *blessings* for those who do.

Lincoln said, "God must love the common man, He made so many of them."

Fortunately for us, He still does. Today, try to be uncommonly common by being humble toward everyone.

Top-Contender

Blessed are you, O Israel!

Deuteronomy 33:29

Israel was the new name given to Jacob by God. It means "He contends with God." Unfortunately, the nation of Israel would really live up to this name. Continuously.

Throughout history, Israel was a nation that almost always frustrated God. The Israelites were obedient only when they had to be or came under severe punishment. When they were prosperous and safe, they saw no need for God.

Because they left Him, He left them, as He had promised He would.

We're just like they were. We have so much that dependence on God for anything sounds old-fashioned. On top of that, we contend with Him daily.

Yet in this verse, God is *blessing* Israel, despite His knowing that they would continue to contend with Him in the future. He knows our future and still blesses us, too.

Contending with God is stupid—just ask Jacob.

Don't be stupid today!

Waiting Game

The fruit of your womb will be *blessed*, and the crops of your land and the young of your livestock—the calves of your herds and the lambs of your flocks.

Deuteronomy 28:4

Faith takes patience. We hope and pray we'll receive the Lord's *blessings* He promised in this verse, but we still have unmet needs. So we wait, pray, wait, pray.

We know God wants only to do good for us and that all of God's promises are ours, but we're never sure what hinders a positive answer to our prayers.

We silently suffer and secretly doubt we'll ever receive what we're begging for. We grow envious of others who seem to "have it all" while we wait and pray.

Instead of doubting, we should remember He loves us and continues to *bless* us in many, many ways, even while we wait in faith for *all our prayers to be answered.*

Remember His love for us as we wait and pray and watch in faith today.

JUNE 1

Half and Half

Half of the people stood in front of Mount
Gerizim and half of them in front of Mount
Ebal, as Moses the servant of the Lord had
formerly commanded when he gave instructions to *bless* the people of Israel.

Joshua 8:33

We'll often give the benefit of the doubt to others. If
someone does us right, we'll feel good about our optimistic decision. If we're done wrong, though, we'll be
angry at them and ourselves.

God is not an optimist; He's a realist. He knows we'll
all continue to sin. In this passage, the obedient half
of the people are uttering *blessings* on the nation, and
the other half, the disobedient, are shouting curses on
themselves.

The blessings endured for a while, but eventually,
the curses came true for Israel.

But then came Jesus: the Way, the Truth, and the
Life.

He died for us; He took the curses and redeemed
us from them.[34] It is guaranteed we'll be disobedient
again, but we'll still be *blessed* nevertheless.

God is a realist and has prepared a Way for our future, which starts today!

Supersize Me

> About Gad he said: *"Blessed* is he who enlarges Gad's domain!"
>
> **Deuteronomy 33:20**

We all want more. A larger home, a bigger bank account, a nicer vacation...it's natural, and not all bad.

In this verse, we see that anyone who helped enlarge the tribe of Gad was *blessed.* Like Gad, we're always working to improve our life and enlarge our own "territory." In the Old Testament, riches were seen as a measure of God's grace. In the New Testament, while God doesn't deny this quest for more, He does want us to keep our perspective.

We're called upon to appreciate Him and to share with others.

The apostle Paul spent much of his time convincing wealthier Christians to share with the poor. Paul prayed that those who did would be *blessed* for their generosity.

It is the *love* of riches that is condemned. If we're honest, most of us don't need more stuff, we need more of God and more love toward others.

Pray for supersized faith today!

Cheer Up

Give generously to them and do so without a
grudging heart; then because of this the Lord
your God will bless you in all your work and in
everything you put your hand to.

Deuteronomy 15:10

Throughout Scripture, we're encouraged to be generous. What we have in the west is much more than
most other people on the planet, and sharing our physical goods with others is a way for us to help, at least
momentarily, those who may be suffering.

We're also supposed to share out of love, not just a
sense of duty. Paul said it best, "God loves a cheerful
giver."[35]

In this verse, God promises to reward our generosity. If we truly believed we'd be greatly *blessed* by unself-
ish giving, we'd do a lot more, wouldn't we?

But our giving has to be done with measures of faith
and love: faith that God will provide for us and genuine
love for the recipients.

When we understand that God will always make
sure we have enough when we share, it will set us free
to give with joy.

Try hard to be a cheerful giver today.

Get Real

After he had finished sacrificing the burnt offerings and fellowship offerings, he *blessed* the people in the name of the Lord Almighty.

2 Samuel 6:18

Ending well sounds good in theory. We want others to see our life as a series of challenges we overcame, which culminates in our quiet passing, with family and friends grieving their great loss.

Nice thought. Let's get real.

We're always struggling in life. Sometimes we're successful, and sometimes we fail miserably. We leave behind some love but also hurt feelings and broken or bruised relationships.

What we should aim for is knowing Jesus more. He is real every moment. We can't fool, flatter or frustrate Him. He's joyful when we're faithful. He is forgiving when we're not. Nothing will be more real than seeing Him live and in person at the finish line.

That is the essence of ending well, and living well, through Him today.

Honest to God

Through the blessing of the upright a city is exalted, but by the mouth of the wicked it is destroyed.

Proverbs 11:11

We're living in a very political world today. Much of what we say and write is continuously measured against some standard that approves or condemns it. Often, our continued membership in a particular group depends on our opinions on a number of topics, ranging from abortion to immigration to gender issues. Some people won't even date someone with the "wrong" views.

God didn't give specific guidance on every current issue.

He did give us His Son.

Jesus's life and words are very clear and honest to those who know Him. Just like someone from Japan understands Japanese, a friend of Jesus can clearly interpret the meaning of His words. His intent is simple: love Him and love each other.

While it may not win an election or an argument, let's be honest to God today.

Nice Neighborhood

It is a sin to despise one's neighbor, but *blessed*
is the one who is kind to the needy.

Proverbs 14:21

These days, the concept of neighbors is changing.
Many people don't know their neighbors and really
don't want to. In a mobile society, it's hard to develop a
deep relationship with anyone. Because renting is popular, the person next door may be gone by the end of the
month. Even homeowners don't socialize frequently. A
simple wave or "Good morning" may be our only social
interaction with our neighbors.

Jesus speaks about neighbors differently. In the parable of the "Good Samaritan,"[36] He makes it clear our
neighbors are the needy, just like this verse suggests.

"Needy" doesn't just mean poor; it can also mean
the insecure, emotionally fragile, and even arrogant. In
other words, they share those traits with us! We're commanded to be kind to everybody, especially the people
we dislike the most.

Many of us have loud, selfish, and obnoxious neighbors, but ask yourself: why are they like that? Could
kindness change them?

Maybe they can do with a little more *blessing* from
us today.

Treasure Hunt

Isaac planted crops in that land and the same
year reaped a hundredfold because the Lord
blessed him.

Genesis 26:12

It is always good to remember God has ultimate control and knows how we will react to various challenges, temptations and blessings. Still, we always like to think we're the ones in control of every aspect of our lives; whatever falls outside of our control, we call luck, either good luck or bad luck.

In this passage, Isaac had an amazing year in farming, with his rate of return being an astounding 100 percent! Most of us would be thrilled with an 8 percent return! Was it good rain, the right fertilizer, or his skill that achieved this remarkable accomplishment? Some would say he was lucky, but we know the truth.

Don't believe in luck; believe in *blessings* by relying on God and pleasing Him. God doesn't bless us because of our works, but our works do open doors for His blessing.

We may not always get a 100 percent return on our investments, but we'll be assured we're storing up treasure in Heaven.

Where will our treasure be kept today: Heaven, or here?

Taste Test

Prepare me the kind of tasty food I like and
bring it to me to eat, so I may give you my
blessing.

Genesis 27:4

The Bible is full of instances involving eating.
Whether it's lamb, goat, beef, fowl, or fish, eating is often part of the scene. Foodies are experts at recognizing the subtleties of obscure dishes, while others are happy to chow down on fast foods daily.

Food plays a huge role in the biblical family of Isaac, Abraham's son. His son, Esau, had a weakness for spicy food; he sold his birthright to his brother for a bowl of stew. Esau's brother, Jacob, prepared a bowl of stew to Esau's tastes and traded it for his birthright; when he went to steal Isaac's blessing, he tricked his father by pretending to be Esau. The discovery of this ruse led to a break-up of that family.

Jesus made it clear that what we eat, drink and wear can be a distraction because those can cause us to focus on our desires, not on loving people.

The Lord has provided food, drink, and clothes in abundance. What we need to develop is love and patience, things usually in very short supply.

How can we focus on others today instead of striving to fulfill our selfish desires?

Freedom Now

Do not consider it a hardship to set your servant free, because their service to you these six years has been worth twice as much as a hired hand. And the Lord will *bless* you in everything you do.

Deuteronomy 15:18

It is sometimes hard to let go. We cry at weddings and funerals because loved ones are departing for a new life. Our hesitation to let go isn't limited to people, either; we all have favorite possessions, from treasured heirlooms to baseball cards.

We cling to these things because they give us some measure of security in an uncertain world.

In this passage, God told the Israelites to release their Jewish slaves every seven years. Slaves were definitely a form of security, however, and a measure of one's wealth.

Regardless, God commanded the Israelites to free their slaves. This obviously involved giving up a large portion of Israelites' property, this was an extreme test of their faith, but God promised He would greatly *bless* them for their obedience.

He'll always *bless* us abundantly when we are obedient to Him, but He also gives us the freedom to ignore Him. What's the plan for today?

R-E-S-P-E-C-T

While the whole assembly of Israel was standing there, the king turned around and *blessed* them.

2 Chronicles 6:3

We like acknowledgment. We seek the respect of our coworkers and employers, and we like to be appreciated when we give a gift. Being complimented on how we look or for something helpful we did feels great, too.

It makes us feel real.

Few things feel worse than being taken for granted or ignored. It is belittling and hurtful because it makes us feel worthless.

In this verse, King Solomon *blesses* the people. He does this out of respect for the people and God. As he was a king, his subjects ranked below him, but he still modeled Jesus's future humility. Jesus likewise accepted people who had been easily neglected.

That's our mission, too.

We're to take Jesus's concern for others to the world and recognize everyone as a potential brother and sister in Him. Jesus's love and acknowledgment of society's underclass extends to us.

Go and do likewise today.

Light-Headed

Blessed are those who have learned to acclaim
You, who walk in the light of Your presence,
O Lord.

Psalm 89:15

Light is essential for seeing. Edison's light bulb changed the world, which means we don't need candles anymore. Seeing ought to be easier than ever, but though some people's eyes work well, they refuse to truly see.

In this Psalm, we're encouraged to walk in the light of God's presence, but His brightness can be overwhelming. God's light reveals things about our heart we'd rather ignore. Still, facing ourselves honestly isn't just enlightening; it's humbling. It is much easier to blame the world for our problems than accept the fact we are to blame, too.

Jesus said we are to let the blind lead the blind.[37]

If we want to see Him, we need to learn to seek God in worship and prayer. Jesus is the light we're looking for.

Pray today that He'll help us see all He has planned for us to do.

Culture Clash

Blessed are you who are poor, for yours is the kingdom of God.

Luke 6:20

We're increasingly becoming a culture of haves and have-nots. Feelings of insecurity and envy often surround us, and when we look into the homes and lifestyles of the rich and famous, it is easy to want what they have. It is even easier to be frustrated at ourselves for not having more.

Life isn't fair, but nobody wants their nose rubbed into their own shortcomings.

Jesus, in this verse, *blesses* the have-nots. Even if we are rich on Earth, we can be in this class of "have-nots" if we realize our whole existence is dependent on Him.

Solomon said the wealthy see their money as a "fortified city"[38] which can dull their need to depend on God. The less fortunate often live on the edge and know their need for His constant mercy and grace.

Live on the edge with faith in Him today.

Poor Taste

He too prepared some tasty food and brought it to his father. Then he said to him, "My father, sit up and eat some of my game, so that you may give me your *blessing*."

Genesis 27:31

We're all living in the past, in the sense that we've made some choices that altered the course of our lives.

In the Bible, Esau and Judas are two of the most tragic figures. Both made decisions that radically changed their lives, and the lives of millions of people after them, forever.

Unfortunately, we have some Judas and Esau in us, too.

We're manipulative, dishonest and treat holy things (like our relationship with God and our neighbors) as a nuisance. We see them as inconveniences or afterthoughts.

Even though God wants us to taste the good things He has prepared for us, we turn up our noses all too often.

Sound familiar?

Make it a daily point today to taste and see that He, and everything and everyone He created, is good.[39]

Father Knows Best

So Isaac called for Jacob and *blessed* him and commanded him: "Do not marry a Canaanite woman."

Genesis 28:1

Giving advice is tricky. We think we have great ideas because we consider ourselves wise and experienced; that's obvious, right? Unfortunately, most people don't want our advice and may resent it. Adult children are strong examples of this. Parents with younger children can make rules and still enforce them, but once they are out of the nest, Mom and Dad's instructions can be easily disregarded (and they often are).

Likewise, God lets us make our own decisions.

He guides us through His word, prayer, the Holy Spirit, and other people, but it's completely up to us to obey or ignore Him. In this passage, Jacob wisely took his father's advice, and because he did, his life (and ours) were changed for the better forever.

Not everything dad or mom advised was right, but advice from our Heavenly Father is always best.

Spending enough time with Him today is the only way to know when He is speaking to us.

JUNE 15

Wild-Eyed Radicals

> Then celebrate the Feast of Weeks to the Lord
> your God by giving a freewill offering in pro-
> portion to the *blessings* the Lord your God has
> given you.
>
> **Deuteronomy 16:10**

Of all the things that require faith, giving may be the hardest. It means taking our hard-earned dollars and using them to *bless* others instead of using the money to cover bills or pay for a well-deserved vacation. Gifting can even mean that money is not set aside for college or retirement, and once it's gone, it is completely out of our control.

That kind of giving sounds radical, but does God think so?

Normal people donate what they can spare. Radicals give without restraint. Jesus commended a widow for giving two coins because that was all she had. She was a radical widow!

Jesus looks at what we give rather than what we keep.

Jesus's death is His radical gift to us.

What sort of radical things should we do today?

Family Resemblance

It is as if the dew of Hermon were falling on Mount Zion. For there the Lord bestows His *blessing*, even life forevermore.

Psalm 133:3

God sometimes refers to physical places when He talks about blessings. His favorite is Jerusalem (Mount Zion is another name for it). No one is sure why God picked Jerusalem: it is not located near a river, it is not on the way to anywhere important, and there have always been more attractive cities.

Maybe that's His point.

God never selects people who have it all together, either. Those people don't need Him. They think they're in control.

The rest of us know we're lacking in physical, financial, emotional, or spiritual resources.

That is why He *blesses* us.

We know we need Him, and He likes to be needed. All of His family members have been humbled. Salvation requires it, so learn to like it!

Jesus said the world will know us by our love for one another, and love takes humility.

How can we act more humbly toward everyone today?

Pile It High

When Hezekiah and his officials came and saw the heaps, they praised the Lord and *blessed* His people Israel.

2 Chronicles 31:8

We never know when we'll be blessed. God likes it that way. He knows what we need, when we need it, and how to deliver it, but He also knows our faith needs to grow, and when a healthy dose of humility is in order.

Unfortunately (or, maybe, fortunately), there are no "magic words" we can recite.

Prayer is personal.

Written or memorized prayers may help us focus, but it is what is in our hearts, not our mouths, that matters.

In this verse, God *blessed* Israel because they finally followed His commands after years of neglecting His instructions. This should give us comfort because they sinned, and so do we. They then prayed, obeyed, and were *blessed*.

Now it's our turn.

Despite Israel's past, He *blessed* them. And it is never too late for us, either.

It starts today!

Share and Share Alike

People curse the one who hoards grain, but they pray God's *blessing* on the one who is willing to sell.

Proverbs 11:26

In the movie *Wall Street*, Gordon Gekko's motto is that "greed is good," and this seems to be our culture's mantra. Our economic system even encourages it, and Solomon himself observed that the desire for "more" motivates us.

That desire is innate. We sometimes hide our pursuit of riches by saying we're doing it for our family's security, but our hearts know we're doing it for ourselves.

Yet, the aftermath of greed can be devastating.

As a good example, in this verse, Solomon complains about someone who doesn't share with the needy. Paul never said money itself was the root of all evil; instead, it is the *love* of money that is the root of all kinds of evil.[40] He said this for two reasons: first, we need to depend on God, not money because He will always provide for us. Second, loving our neighbor requires that we share with others.

Having is different to hoarding. What we have, we're supposed to share. It is as simple as that.

What can we share with someone today?

JUNE 19

Life and Death

After Abraham's death, God *blessed* his son,
Isaac, who then lived near Beer Lahai Roi.
Genesis 25:11

Life and death seem to be opposites: life is supposed
to be positive and exciting, but thoughts of death are
depressing and sad. Really, though, they are just different
ends along the same spectrum.

Families are strong examples of this.

We're all born into a family that's imperfect, and the
relationships within that family are sometimes complex
and frustrating. If step-family members join, the
dynamic changes even more.

The point is that families are always changing: kids
grow up, grandchildren are born, and grandparents
die.

After Abraham died, God *blessed* Isaac because his
father had successfully passed down the knowledge
and love of God to him. It didn't matter that Abraham
was his father; it was Isaac's personal faith and love for
God that counted.

It also doesn't matter what family we're born into. If
we have our own faith in God, we'll be *blessed* with eternal
life. We can't get to God through our parents' faith;
it must be our one-on-one relationship with God.

Reflect on this because God doesn't have grandchildren,
only sons and daughters.

Will others recognize that we're part of His family
by the way we act today?

Food Fight

Then take it to your father to eat, so that he
may give you his *blessing* before he dies.

Genesis 27:10

For the first time in history, Americans spend more
money at restaurants than at grocery stores.[41]

This could be a sign we enjoy eating too much,
which means we end up fighting or giving in to urges
of gluttony. Appropriately enough, the dieting industry
makes billions of dollars each year, helping people fight
the weight gained from too much eating.

In this verse, Jacob used food to deceive his father
into blessing him over his brother, Esau.

Esau should have received the *blessing* because he
was Isaac's oldest son, but God allowed Jacob to receive
the *blessing*. This is because Esau sold the treasure of his
birthright to Jacob for a simple bowl of stew.

Esau chose physical comfort over spiritual *blessings*.

Will our daily choices today be centered on spiritual
blessings or temporary comforts?

End Game

May God *bless* us still, so that all the ends of
the earth will fear him.

Psalm 67:7

We're always seeking security, so we plan for retirement and vote for candidates who we hope will keep us safe. For our children, we do everything we can, short of dressing them in bubble-wrap, to keep them from harm. Our national defense budget is massive, and we pay huge insurance premiums just in case there is a catastrophe.

Yet, none of this is guaranteed to keep us safe: Christ is our only real security.

In this verse, the prayer is that God will *bless* us so that everyone on Earth will acknowledge Him when they see His blessings on us. The fear of God's power is like our approach to electricity: it is a valuable resource, and we depend on it, and we treat it with respect. When others see God's *blessings* on us, they may decide to choose a relationship with Him, too.

We are all writing our life stories, but God gets to write the ending for each of us.

Let's do our best today to make our end game a happy one.

Stand Up

While the whole assembly of Israel was standing there, the king turned around and *blessed* them.

1 Kings 8:14

Standing up in someone's presence is a show of respect. In some cultures, standing up is reserved for dignitaries, while in others, people stand up merely when a new person enters the room. Some people stand when praying, and others kneel down. Protestants very rarely kneel, and Catholics kneel many times during Mass. We follow the traditions we are taught as children, and in turn, our children learn them by watching us.

The assembly of Israel stood while the Ark of the Covenant was being placed in Solomon's temple. They were standing to show respect for God.

God is not overly concerned with our traditions, but He is greatly concerned with our hearts. Whether standing, kneeling, or sitting, the point is to honor and love God because He values a spiritual perspective over a physical position.

How can we show our reverence for God today?

Day Two

On the following day he sent the people away. They *blessed* the king and then went home, joyful and glad in heart for all of the good things the Lord had done for his servant David and his people Israel.

1 Kings 8:66

Emotions on the second day of any event are different from the first. Day one is full of excitement and anticipation. On the second day, our expectations may have been fulfilled, but often, we may feel disappointed.

Day two is a reality check. We take stock of what happened and decide whether it was worth the effort, time, and investment.

On day one, Solomon dedicated God's temple in Jerusalem; on day two, everyone had a feast. They were delighted because they'd experienced God and had seen His glory fill the new temple.

Some days, we enjoy the excitement of experiencing God, but on our second day, we often struggle getting through the turmoil of our daily lives. He wants to live in our hearts and provides joy and gladness minute-by-minute, not just on day two, three, or four. How much time will we spend with God today?

Sleight of Hand

"No, my son," the king replied. "All of us should not go; we would only be a burden to you." Although Absalom urged him, he still refused to go, but he gave him his *blessing*.

2 Samuel 13:25

We're all being manipulated constantly. College students major in marketing so they can share in the $600 billion spent annually on advertising. Politicians run misleading campaigns to get votes, and we are talked into and out of many things for other people's benefit.

Sleight of hand is a powerful tool.

Although Absalom invited his father to a celebration, he knew King David wouldn't attend. He was manipulating David so that he would send Absalom's brother, Amnon, instead. Absalom's goal was to murder Amnon because he had attacked their sister.

We also manipulate people, whether through guilt, shouting, tears, or little bribes. God doesn't work that way, He loves us and wants us to obey Him because we love Him back.

We can't manipulate God, and we shouldn't manipulate others.

Today just try to love them all.

Shining Star

I will make your descendants as numerous
as the stars in the sky and will give them all
these lands, and through your offspring all
nations on earth will be *blessed*.

Genesis 26:4

Science allows us to view the farthest reaches of the
universe, but no one knows how many stars there are in
the sky, and we probably never will.

Yet that's the *blessing* God is promising to Isaac.

The promise wasn't limited to Isaac's two sons. It
was meant for all of us through one specific descendant
of Abraham: Jesus. The *blessing* is for everyone who follows Isaac's God, but He needs us to share this good
news by the lives we live as examples to those around
us.

We are not able to personally reach all the nations on
Earth, but if we each do our part, we will multiply.

How can God's blessing shine through us today?

Don't Go There

But God said to Balaam, "Do not go with them. You must not put a curse on those people, because they are *blessed*."

Numbers 22:12

We always seem to be on the move. If we work, we have a commute, and even if we don't work, we still have seemingly endless errands to run. Retired people often say, "Do everything you want to do before you retire because when you finally do retire, you won't have the time to do anything."

The prophet Balaam was asked to curse Israel by the enemies of the Israelites, but he was commanded by God not to go and do so. We're also frequently told not to go somewhere or to avoid situations, whether it's a confrontation, a bad attitude, or yielding to sin. Later in this passage, we learn that Balaam nearly died at the hands of a holy angel because he was disobedient to the command he received in this verse.

The Holy Spirit and wise, godly friends often advise us as to where we shouldn't go and what we shouldn't do. There is no shortage of temptations.

Staying put could be the best move we make today.

Backfire

Balak said to Balaam, "What have you done to me? I brought you to curse my enemies, but you have done nothing but *bless* them!"

Numbers 23:11

Things often don't turn out as we expect: the career we chose isn't fulfilling, the person we love isn't perfect, and what we had dreamed and hoped for hasn't happened. While planning our future carefully is the smart thing to do, we must remember that God is always in ultimate control.

Balak had paid Balaam a large fee to curse the people of Israel. Instead, Balaam couldn't help but repeatedly bless them. Balak's plan backfired because neither he nor Balaam was in control of *blessing* or cursing God's people.

God was.

We can curse ourselves by deliberately sinning, but Jesus's death on the cross made sure even our self-destructive actions will be forgiven if we repent.

If we do, we will continue to be *blessed*.

And the best way to bring *blessing* upon ourselves is by blessing others today.

Facts Are Facts

Moses and Aaron then went into the tent of
meeting. When they came out, they *blessed*
the people; and the glory of the Lord appeared
to all the people.

Leviticus 9:23

In this verse, the Israelites had been camped in the
desert for a year. They didn't like it, and who could
blame them? Moses and Aaron had just been told by
God to bless the people, and so they did. God then
showed His glory to all the people gathered around that
tent, and they shouted for joy at the sight.

How *blessed* they must have felt.

God *blesses* us constantly, too, but we miss ninety-
eight percent of those *blessings* because we attribute
them to luck, coincidence, or our own wise choices.

The Israelites later rebelled against God and Moses
because they weren't happy with God being in charge.
They wanted to control their own destinies.

Does this sound familiar? We want to control our
own future, but God is always in control.

The Israelites didn't like it, and we may not either...
but facts are facts.

Remember that today when someone says they were
"lucky."

Fast Friends

So all the people crossed the Jordan, and then the king crossed over. The king kissed Barzillai and gave him his *blessing*, and Barzillai returned to his home.

2 Samuel 19:39

In America, we don't emphasize formality as much as some other cultures do. In many cultures, a kiss on the cheek shows respect; in some countries, like Japan, they greet each other with a bow, and a lower and longer bow shows greater respect. In North America, however, a head nod or handshake is an appropriate form of greeting.

In this verse, King David is returning to Israel after a victory over his son Absalom, who planned to destroy him. Barzillai risked his family and his fortune by being loyal to the king, despite the rebellion that could have swept him away.

Are we loyal in the same way to our great King, Jesus? We don't have to kneel, bow, or fall face down to acknowledge our Savior. We just need to love Him and love one another.

What are we willing to risk for our King today?

Rainy Day

About Joseph he said: "May the Lord *bless* his land with the precious dew from heaven above and with the deep waters that lie below."

Deuteronomy 33:13

We love rain when it waters our plants and fills our reservoirs, yet we dislike it when we're on vacation or when it creates floods. The Israelites would normally get showers in season, but God promised He would withhold the rain when they had sinned or rebelled against Him.

Here, the land of Joseph's tribe is being *blessed* with the promise of abundant water resources.

This was a great *blessing* in a semi-arid region.

Sadly, Joseph's tribe later forfeited this blessing by abandoning God for idols. Our *blessings* can be forfeited too if we follow after the false gods like envy, materialism, greed, and pride. God used rain to *bless* the Israelites and to correct them.

The blessings we receive can be delayed or accelerated, depending on our level of devotion to Him.

How devout will we be today?

Big Time

They took palm branches and went out to meet Him, shouting, "Hosanna! Blessed is He who comes in the name of the Lord."

John 12:13

For some people "hitting the big" time means a huge business opportunity; for others, it's fantastic fame. For others still, it signifies something bigger than ourselves, a purpose larger than life.

Here, Jesus's coming to town was the big time for Jerusalem. They expected Jesus to overcome the Roman army, maybe even topple the whole empire and be crowned king. Jesus knew what was to come and that this was the fulfillment of prophecies. Still, Jesus's ego didn't need any massaging, so He entered Jerusalem humbly, riding on a donkey.

We're usually not like Him in this way, are we?

We love being acknowledged for what we do, and we can be resentful when we aren't. When we recognize this, we should pray for humility and realize being humble is what hitting the big time really means.

Then we have to remember not to become proud of our humility!

The only prayer God will *always* answer is a prayer for humility.

Pray for more of that today.

Golden Years

Now then, my children, listen to me; *blessed* are those who keep my ways.

Proverbs 8:32

Parenting ought to be easier. There are hundreds of books on the subject, and well-meaning friends and family always have tons of unsolicited advice. TV families seem to have it all figured out, so what's the problem?

The problem is that imperfect parents are trying hard to raise perfect children who, no matter how much teaching and guidance they receive, will be imperfect, too.

Here, Solomon is trying to do one of the most difficult jobs of any parent, and that is giving an adult child advice. For parents, the real golden years are when the child is young enough to be told what to do and actually have to do it! Children remain our children no matter how old they are, however; and God wants us to continue guiding them even when they are older and even when they do not want that guidance (which is often!).

It is our job to guide our family, coworkers, and friends closer to Him.

Are you up for that today?

Snipe Hunt

Isaac trembled violently and said, "Who was
it, then, that hunted the game and brought
it to me? I ate it just before you came and I
blessed him—and indeed he will be *blessed*!"

Genesis 27:33

A snipe hunt is a practical joke played on unsuspecting people. It involves a hike to find "snipes" that the so-called experienced hikers see and encourage the first-time hikers to see, too.

But they're deceiving the new hikers: the snipes are imaginary.

In this passage, Isaac went snipe hunting; Jacob fooled his father into giving him his older brother Esau's *blessing*.

We go on snipe hunts all the time. The snipes may be wealth, possessions, status, or wandering away from Biblical truth to a more "universalist" view that all good people get to Heaven.

The victims of snipe hunts always feel foolish when they realize they have been duped, but to be the victim of a spiritual snipe hunt is ultimately disastrous.

Be careful of snipe hunts that will lead you away from God's truth today.

All Grown up

Your descendants will be like the dust of the earth, and you will spread out to the west and to the east, to the north and to the south. All peoples on earth will be *blessed* through you and your offspring.

Genesis 28:14

We are all growing things, even if we don't realize it. If we have young children, we want them to grow physically and intellectually, so we feed them properly and educate them as best we can. A gardener's joy is watching what was planted grow to produce flowers or fruit. Likewise, a career needs nurturing to thrive, too.

In this scripture, God promises to grow Jacob's family, spread them across the world, and *bless* everyone on Earth through his offspring. God is always faithful to His word, and today, counting all the Jewish people born since Jacob would be like trying to count the sand on any beach.

The *blessing* God promises the world through Jacob is Jesus, a descendant of Jacob, who came to show us God's love and save the world from sin.

Jesus said He is the vine and we are the branches, and if we consistently follow Him, we will bear plenty of fruit in our lives. He also said if we stop following Him, we are like branches that wither and die and are cut off and thrown into the fire.

How can we be more fruitful today?

The Winning Margin

If you are insulted for the name of Christ, you are *blessed*, for the Spirit of glory and of God rests on you.

1 Peter 4:14

No one enjoys being insulted or ridiculed, yet daily we have to put up with it in some way. It may be an ungrateful boss, a loved one who takes us for granted, or another driver who cuts us off. We try to minimize insult and pain, but if we're living for God, we'll find it everywhere we go.

Peter knew the pain of rejecting Jesus when He was at His worst suffering. Peter is warning us that Christians will always be insulted for our faith in God because society increasingly marginalizes our values and beliefs. He is telling us to be ready and to rest in God's glory and peace when we are insulted for Him.

God wins in the end, and we will too if we stick with Him today.

Dress for Success

The young women saw her and called her
blessed...

Song of Solomon 6:9

Society puts amazing emphasis on how we look. Our appearance can influence how people treat us, whether we get the job we want or how much attention we get from waiters or store clerks.

Fashion has always been important to society, but notice how older people pay less attention to fashion and trends: they have learned it's mostly superficial.

Here, Solomon's bride is praised for her beauty. She didn't hide it, but she stayed humble through all the attention. We need to dress well for work and special occasions, but our real beauty is displaying Jesus's life within us.

Today remember to dress, walk, and talk in ways that please and uplift Him; the value of a book is in the pages, not the cover.

Count Your Blessings

That night the Lord appeared to him and said,
"I am the God of your father Abraham. Do not
be afraid, for I am with you; I will *bless* you
and will increase the number of your descendants for the sake of my servant Abraham."

Genesis 26:24

More often than not, we don't hear God when He
speaks; better yet, we don't *listen* to Him. People think if
we listen too well, God will send us to some third world
country as a missionary to spend the rest of our lives in
misery and poverty.

In this verse, Isaac is *blessed* because he is listening
to God, just like his father Abraham did. God didn't
send him into a black hole; He *blessed* him by increasing
his family to the point that they became a nation.

God speaks to us because He loves us and has a plan
for our lives, a plan just as important as the plan He had
for Abraham and Isaac.

If we just listen to Him today, who knows how richly
God will *bless* us?

Deep Breathing

So he went to him and kissed him. When Isaac
caught the smell of his clothes, he *blessed* him
and said, "Ah, the smell of my son is like the
smell of a field that the Lord has *blessed*."

Genesis 27:27

The sense of smell is powerful. It might seem to be
the least important of the senses, but it helps us decide
which foods to eat and which ones to avoid. A mother
even recognizes the smell of her baby.

Here, Jacob used the scent of his brother Esau's
clothes to trick his father into giving him the *blessing*.
Isaac knew his son, Esau's scent, just as God knows
ours. Still, Isaac was tricked, but we can't trick God, nor
can we hide our sins.

Sin stinks, but Jesus's blood washes our sins away.
Breathe that fact in today.

Peace in Our Time

> They answered, "We saw clearly that the
> Lord was with you; so we said, 'There ought
> to be a sworn agreement between us'—be-
> tween us and you. Let us make a treaty with
> you that you will do us no harm, just as we
> did not harm you but always treated you well
> and sent you away in peace. And now you are
> *blessed* by the Lord."
>
> **Genesis 26:28-29**

We need peace in different ways at different times. Some wish for peace in their family, while others need to find peace with themselves. To live in a period of peace is a blessing that often only people who have lived through a war can appreciate.

Maintaining peace in a world where everybody looks out for themselves is difficult. God tells us not to worry about anything, trust Him, and He will give us the peace that passes all understanding.[42]

Here, Isaac's more powerful neighbors who had been fighting with him are trying to make peace because they saw he had God's *blessing*. We, too, can live in peace with our neighbors, family, and even those we don't get along with because we also have God's *blessing*.

We all want peace in the world, so let's do our part. Mother Teresa said it best: "Peace begins with a smile."

Smile more today.

Open House

Blessed is he who comes in the Name of the Lord. From the house of the Lord we bless you.

Psalm 118:26

An open house can mean several things. It can refer to a party where people come and go, or it can mean a home being shown to the public in hopes of attracting a buyer. The important word here is "open." Normally we like privacy, especially in our homes, but an open house is usually an invitation to come in and explore.

God wants that type of relationship with us. He wants us to be curious about Him and to explore His world. He wants us to invite Him into our house so He can *bless* us from His house.

Don't lock Him out today; just open the door. He's there waiting.

Truth Squad

Blessed is the land whose king is of noble birth
and whose princes eat at the proper time—
for strength and not for drunkenness.

Ecclesiastes 10:17

We have lost our sense of nobility over the last few generations. In the past, hard work, respect for others, and dignified behavior were valued in society. We've long since traded that for popularity and fads. Many of the media icons most envied today are crude, rude, and unstable. They have influence because society has lost much of its ability to distinguish between good and bad messages and ideas.

Sadly, the more outrageous today's "idols" are, the greater their following.

While the world around us may be changing, Jesus never changes. His message has stayed the same for two thousand years. He came to show us the way to God and save us from false messages that lead to failure. Let's look past all the messages the world is trying to force on us and follow the Son, who is the same yesterday, today, and forever.

Jesus, our great and noble King, is the truth, the whole truth and nothing but the truth, today and always.

Raise 'em High

Then Aaron lifted his hands toward the people and *blessed* them.

Leviticus 9:22

Lifted hands is a universal symbol of praise and unity. The Bible uses the term "lifted" many times when offerings are presented to God. This is because God's home is in Heaven, and that is where our focus should be.

Here, Aaron was giving his very first *blessing* to the Israelites. Bear in mind, he had previously failed God by creating the golden calf for them to worship when he wasn't sure if Moses was going to return from Mount Sinai. God forgave him and still made him the high priest of Israel.

God forgives us when we make mistakes, too. He picks us up and *blesses* us, even though we don't deserve it. So, let's raise our hands and praise Him.

Like children raise their arms when they want to be picked up, let's lift our arms to our Heavenly Father.

He's ready to *bless* us, too.

No Place Like Home

Now, be pleased to *bless* the house of Your servant, that it may continue forever in Your sight.

2 Samuel 7:29

In *The Wizard of Oz*, Dorothy said, "There's no place like home," and she was right! Our home is the place we feel safe and comfortable. When someone says, "I feel at home with my surroundings," they mean it as a state of mind.

Home, however, can also be a spiritual place. Older people sometimes say they're "ready to go home."

In this verse, "house" means a family lineage. God told David He would build him a family line that would last forever. David wondered whether he was worthy of this *blessing* on his house when he said, "Who am I, Lord, and what is my family, that you have brought me this far?"[43]

Most of us feel we deserve God's *blessings* without even thinking about why.

Whatever our home may be to us, do we take God's blessings on our home for granted?

Today focus on our ultimate Heavenly home; don't get too comfortable down here in this fallen world.

Topsy-Turvy

Blessed is the coming kingdom of our father,
David! Hosanna in the highest!

Mark 11:10

At reunions, we get to connect with friends and
family we haven't seen in a long time. They give us the
opportunity to share old stories again and catch up on
what's new. They're joyous occasions, except when remembering those who are missing the get-together.

Here, Jesus's arrival in Jerusalem was the ultimate
reunion. Just like David, He was the long-awaited new
King, but in just five days, the same crowd that wel-
comed His arrival would shout for His crucifixion.

Jesus went from the top of their list to the bottom in
the blink of an eye.

In this flaky and inconsistent world, our situation
can change just as fast. Life is always topsy-turvy, and
trusting in ourselves and other people is very dangerous. We can only put our trust in Jesus because He has
planned a huge reunion in Heaven for His friends who
trust Him.

Topsy-turvy can lead to nausea. Today, don't get on
the roller coaster of life without asking Jesus for more
of His calming presence.

Mother's Day

In a loud voice she exclaimed, *"Blessed* are you among women and *blessed* is the Child you will bear!"

Luke 1:42

We may have the faith to believe God will do what we ask of Him, but faith takes patience. We complain about waiting too long at a drive-through restaurant or in the line at the pharmacy. We want everything now, chop-chop, but often our impatient attitudes cause us to miss the *blessings* right in front of us!

The Jewish people waited about four thousand years for the Messiah, but when He came, few recognized Him.

In this verse, Elizabeth is greeting Mary, Jesus's mother. She knew Mary carried the Savior, but neither of them held a news conference or leaked the story. Mary was *blessed* among women for her faith and obedience to God. She knew that having a baby before she was properly married would ruin her reputation among her people. Worst of all, she knew she would probably lose the man she was promised to marry and could be stoned to death.

But Mary trusted God to work things out for her, and He did in a major way. She received a tremendous *blessing*, being the mother of the world's Savior.

Patience is a virtue. Pray for a lot more of it today.

Grudge Match

Esau held a grudge against Jacob because of
the blessing his father had given him.

Genesis 27:41

When someone wrongs us, holding a grudge against
them can feel right and good. If someone has mistreat-
ed, shamed, or insulted us, our knee-jerk reaction is
resolving to get back at them, one way or another. If
we get the opportunity, we'll try to even the score with
them. If that's not possible, we may start a smear cam-
paign against them. When it's a close family member,
we can always give them the silent treatment and not
acknowledge their existence.

Grudges are emotionally draining and can cause
permanent harm to us and innocent people who aren't
involved. Holding a grudge doesn't solve the problem,
either. A phrase attributed to Anne Lamott says, "Not
forgiving is like drinking rat poison and then waiting
for the rat to die."

We have all sinned against God and need forgiveness. Jesus told us if we do not forgive others for their
sins, our Father will not forgive ours.[44]

Drop any grudges, and instead, pick up the Bible
today.

Shut Up

Then Balak said to Balaam, "Neither curse
them at all nor *bless* them at all!"

Numbers 23:25

Nobody likes bad news; in fact, we'll go to great
lengths to avoid it. Not returning phone calls or e-mails
from upset customers or family members is a cop-out,
but we hope that by pushing the unpleasantness off, it
will go away. We can have the same reaction to a jury
summons and credit card bills.

Here, King Balak hired Balaam, the prophet, to curse
the Israelites as they approached his country. He was
frightened by their numbers and the rumor that God
fought for them.

But Balaam had bad news for Balak, he could only
bless them.

Despite the bad news we may receive, God looks after us. He's in control of the outcome. He *blessed* Israel
despite their sins, and He'll *bless* us despite ours, too.

Remember what Solomon said: "Even a fool who
keeps silent is considered wise."[45]

Try to shut up and just listen to Him today.

Inherited Wealth

Save Your people and *bless* Your inheritance;
be their shepherd and carry them forever.
Psalm 28:9

We inherit all kinds of things from our parents and
grandparents. Genes determine our hair color, eye
color, height, and certain medical conditions, too. The
same goes for our temperaments; they also seem to follow family lines.

Some people inherit family money as well as genetic
traits, but even they can't control any of it. The genes
are set, temperaments are what they are, and the money may be spent before it gets to us.

Jesus talks a lot about inheritances. He said the
meek will inherit the Earth[46] and that His followers will
inherit eternal life.[47] James says those poor in the eyes
of the world but rich in faith will inherit the kingdom
of God.[48] Generally, only blood relatives get an inheritance, but we can be adopted into God's family.

All we have to do is ask Jesus to be our Lord and Savior and live for Him.

Today try to be meek, humble, and poor in the eyes
of the world; eternal life awaits.

Watch Your Back

But he said, "Your brother came deceitfully
and took your *blessing*."

Genesis 27:35

"Watch your back" and "got your back" mean two
very different things. "Watch your back" means you
have to watch out for an attack from behind. "Got your
back" means you will be protected from an attack from
behind.

In Ephesians, Paul tells us to put on the full armor of
God,[49] but most of the pieces of armor he lists protect
the front of our bodies and our heads. What about our
backs?

The answer is simple: we are to never turn our back
and run from a spiritual challenge. When we face it,
whatever it may be, God's got our back!

In this verse, a brother lied his way into receiving his
father's *blessing*. Paul also said that a part of our spiritual armor is the "breastplate of righteousness," and
any deceit in us puts holes in our breastplate, leaving
us open to attack.

Satchel Paige said, "Don't look back. Someone may
be gaining on you." Good advice.

No matter what we've done in the past, Jesus has our
back. Today, He wants us to focus on how we can love
Him and others better.

Separation Anxiety

Then Moses said, "You have been set apart to
the Lord today, for you were against your own
sons and brothers, and He has *blessed* you this
day."

Exodus 32:29

We all want to be part of a group, whether it's a club,
political party, or church. Belonging makes us feel like
we're part of something bigger, but all groups have
written and unwritten rules, requirements, and expectations of their members. Not being part of one can
seem very lonely. Jesus often used flocks of sheep to il-
lustrate how we interact together.

The Levites in this scripture were one of the twelve
Israelite tribes. They defended God's honor after many
of the other Israelites had worshiped a golden statue of
a calf. The Levites were so devout, they went throughout the camp and killed the idol worshipers, whether
they were strangers or close family.

God *blessed* the Levites for their loyalty to Him, and
He'll do the same for us. We don't need to kill idolaters,
but we do need to kill idolatry in our personal life. Jesus
said if we disown Him before others, He will disown us
before the Father.

Rather than hate or kill the idolatrous of this world,
Jesus has commanded us to help bring His lost sheep
into His flock.

How can we find new recruits to join Jesus's flock
today?

Parent Trap

There are those who curse their fathers and
do not *bless* their mothers.

Proverbs 30:11

All parents aren't created equal. Most try to be good
parents, but it's not easy. We all have parents, and many
of us are parents, so we at least know a little about it.
The primary goal of parenting is to help children become successful adults by preparing them to face the
world on their own.

Successful parenting can vary from helping children
mature and establish their own happy families to doing
everything possible to keep them away from drugs and
jail.

Parenting is often a thankless task, and teenagers,
in particular, will sometimes shun their family and
make life hard for everyone.

In the same way, God is *our* parent, and we are the
thankless children. Yet He loves us in our ungrateful-
ness like any parent loves their child. Just like a parent,
He may apply discipline when needed, but only in love
and with our greater future in mind.

When it comes to God, it is never the parent who is
the problem; it is always the children.

Is today the day to leave childish ways behind?

Easy Money

A faithful person will be richly *blessed*, but one eager to get rich will not go unpunished.

Proverbs 28:20

"Get rich quick" books are everywhere! In fact, the fastest way to get rich quickly may be to write one and sell it to poor suckers. Still, wanting more than we have is natural, and pretending not to care about money is almost always a lie.

We all do.

We need money to live and provide for our family, but when we start to love money and chase after more and more, it becomes very dangerous.

In this verse, Solomon tells us a desire for money can be a trap. The Beatles song "Can't Buy Me Love" says it all. Having more can mean having less if it takes us away from our family, friends, and faith. Sadly, it is often the case that the more we have, the less we think we need God.

The reason it is hard for a rich person to get into Heaven is they begin to put their faith in themselves and their money and no longer in God.

Jesus told us to seek first God's kingdom and His righteousness, and all the things we need will be given to us.[50]

What is the most important task to accomplish today?

Chance of Showers

I will send down showers in season; there will
be showers of *blessing*.

Ezekiel 34:26

In dry climates, rain is always a blessing. Rain is so
precious that dams and reservoirs are built at great effort and cost to ensure that they catch every drop.

The climate in Israel is dry, but in this verse, rain
wasn't the problem: the Israelites were dry from a lack
of the word of God. The Babylonians had sacked Jerusalem, and virtually all of the Israelites had been killed
or taken captive. They had rebelled against God by worshipping false gods, and then they suffered the promised, terrible penalty.

Still, Israel had served their time in captivity and
learned their lesson, so God was promising to return
them to their land and shower *blessings* on them again.

We often run spiritually dry too. The reservoir of
our soul is only refilled by praying daily, reading Scripture, and *blessing* others. In this way, we are obeying the
commandments of loving God and loving others.

Is the tank full or empty today?

Count On It

Blessed is the one whose sin the Lord does not count against them and in whose spirit is no deceit.

Psalm 32:2

We often deceive people, even when we don't mean to. We say we're fine when we feel awful, or we tell them we will be there in five minutes when we know it will take us fifteen.

We tell "white lies" to cover for others or to make ourselves look better.

In this scripture, David is making two points. The first is that we all sin, but thankfully, through Jesus's sacrifice on the cross, our sins are forgiven and don't count against us.

The second point David is making is God *detests* deceit. The Bible is full of examples of God's disgust for cheats and liars. While we may continue to sin, we should strive to stop our deceptive ways. Being honest in our dealings with others is not only good business, it's also required if we want God's *blessing*.

God *blesses* honesty. Is that something we can commit to doing all day long today?

JULY 25

From Sea to Shining Sea

Blessed is the nation whose God is the Lord;
the people He chose for His inheritance.

Psalm 33:12

Patriotism runs deep in our country. It is popular to honor the flag and to honor veterans, but it can sometimes become controversial. We'd like to think we're God's chosen people and that this is the Promised Land, but while that's a nice thought, in the Bible, the Promised Land isn't in North America.

Here, the psalmist is speaking about Israel, God's first chosen people. The Bible says they weren't chosen on merit; instead, they were chosen just because He loved them. Now, after Jesus's death on the cross, He also will always love those who believe in the salvation He offers through belief in Jesus's divinity and sacrifice.

Regardless, if more of us submit to Jesus and follow His example, our country will be a much closer picture of Heaven.

Believers are citizens of God's kingdom, and once we're citizens of Heaven, we can't be deported or evicted.

We only rent our place here; we'll own our place there.

Don't let political opinions and turmoil take the focus off of Jesus today.

Easy Credit

You may charge a foreigner interest, but not
a fellow Israelite, so that the Lord your God
may *bless* you in everything you put your hand
to in the land you are entering to possess.

Deuteronomy 23:20

Easy credit sounds good. It means we're able to borrow more money despite our poor credit score. We can
then buy our first (or a bigger) house, drive a nicer car,
and refinance older loans. It is great until the economy
tanks, and then we may lose it all.

God always cares about everything concerning us,
including our finances. He knows we'll be tempted
to over-borrow, and He knows interest payments can
quickly get out of hand. Because of this, He even commanded all debts Israelites owed each other to be can-
celed every seven years.

God's love is astounding. He faithfully cares about
everything, even how we manage our money.

Focus on carefully managing the money He gives us
today.

Filled to the Brim

From the fullness of His grace we have all received one *blessing* after another.

John 1:16

Is the glass half-full or half-empty? Optimists say it is half-full because they see life as positive and expect good things to follow. Pessimists say it is half-empty and that life isn't great and is not likely to improve.

This verse says we receive one *blessing* after another, which tells us if we're the glass, we are to be filled up with God continually. It seems that pessimists choose to cover the top of the glass so they can't be filled up and then say, "See, I was right."

God's Word tells us He gives rain to the good and the bad, to those who want it and those who don't. He blesses us all; some people recognize the *blessings*, and others don't.

If we take stock of all the goodness in our lives, we'll seek God to continually fill our glass to the brim with His presence.

Look for His *blessings* everywhere today.

Laying Blame

The righteous lead blameless lives; *blessed* are
their children after them.

Proverbs 20:7

Nobody likes getting blamed for something going
wrong. When we're criticized, we usually deny the fault
was ours. If we did screw-up, we try to make excuses to
shift the blame. We accuse politicians of being good at
blame-shifting, but if we're honest, we all do it.

This verse comes with a promise: if we're blameless,
our children will be *blessed*.

God knows all of our thoughts, attitudes, and motives. He knows we alone are responsible for our sins,
big and little, and we deserve the consequences. Thankfully, Jesus took the blame for us on the cross, and we
can now be truly blameless. All we have to do is accept
Jesus's sacrifice as fact, acknowledge Him as our Savior
and strive to stop sinning.

Then, even though we deserve the blame, He'll call
us blameless, and we'll be *blessed*!

Today, let's stop blaming ourselves and accept Jesus's grace instead.

Trick or Treat

What if my father touches me? I would appear
to be tricking him and would bring down a
curse on myself rather than a *blessing*.

Genesis 27:12

We're often our own worst enemy when it comes to
our relationships. We harm them by saying things that
make us feel better. You know, we're often more polite
to total strangers than those closest to us.

This verse is an example of Jacob being his own
worst enemy. He's worried about being caught tricking
his father, Isaac. God had mercy on him, but unfortunately, it took his brother, Esau, many, many years to
forgive him.

All too often, we manipulate. While we may not deliberately trick people, we manipulate, we try guilt trips,
and we passively threaten others all too often. Manipulation is a symptom of pride. Let's treat those closest to
us with humility rather than tricking them.

Do today what Jesus commanded: treat people with
love, and don't trick, manipulate or threaten them.

JULY 30

Ugly as Sin

We also know that the law is made not for
the righteous but for lawbreakers and rebels,
the ungodly and sinful, the unholy and irre-
ligious; for those who kill their fathers and
mothers, for murderers, for adulterers and
perverts, for slave traders and liars and per-
jurers—for whatever else is contrary to sound
doctrine that conforms to the glorious gospel
of the *blessed* God, which He entrusted to me.

1 Timothy 1:11

Sin is always ugly. We try to dress it up by telling
ourselves everybody does it, or no one is being harmed
by it. The popular phrase "putting lipstick on a pig" describes this reasoning well: our sin is the pig, and our
excuses are the lipstick.

In this letter to Timothy, Paul is calling us all out. We
may not be murderers and slave traders, but because
we sin we're all lawbreakers and rebels. This means our
sin may not directly harm others, but it always harms
us.

Our redemption is in Jesus alone.

Only He can remove the ugliness of our sin.

Take off the fake lipstick today, and get real with
God and everyone else.

Safekeeping

The Lord *bless* you and keep you.

Numbers 6:24

We spend enormous amounts of time and money trying to keep our family and possessions safe. Locks are just the simplest example of this quest. Some people live in gated communities, our accounts and computers have encryption and passwords, and governments and companies spend billions of dollars annually to keep their data safe.

In this verse, the Lord is directing Moses to *bless* Israel. The Lord had already conveyed His love for them through miracles, but now He wanted to do so in words.

God has the same words of love and *blessing* for us, and with those words, He guides us and keeps us safe from sin and stupidity.

Are we willing to accept His advice, though? The only string attached is that we obey Him and believe in His son Jesus as our Savior.

Today remember that God's security system requires no locks, gates, or passwords, and it has only one key, Jesus.

Divide and Conquer

> When Joshua sent them home, he *blessed* them, saying, "Return to your homes and with your great wealth—with large herds of livestock, with silver, gold, bronze and iron, and with a great quantity of clothing—and divide the plunder from your enemies with your fellow Israelites."
>
> **Joshua 22:7-8**

We're taught to share at an early age because, at our core, we're selfish. A two-year-old believes everything is "mine," and even as adults, we sometimes have to be persuaded or threatened to part with our money. Tithing and taxes are examples of this.

Here, the Israelite army was returning home after conquering the Promised Land. They were rich, but wealth doesn't make people more generous—we hardly ever feel like we have enough.

Managing wealth is a major distraction to our focus on God and His ways. Jesus told a young man who obeyed all the commandments to give everything he had to the poor and follow Him. Jesus then promised the man he would receive treasure in Heaven. The young man went away sad because he had great wealth.[51] He valued his wealth on Earth over the promise of much greater treasure in Heaven.

By dividing and sharing with others, our selfishness and greed can be conquered today.

Choose Wisely

> Now Esau learned that Isaac had *blessed* Jacob and had sent him to Paddan Aram to take a wife from there, and that when he *blessed* him he commanded him, "Do not marry a Canaanite woman."
>
> **Genesis 28:6**

We make big and small decisions daily. The seemingly small decisions can sometimes affect our lives much more than bigger ones, but all of our decisions have an influence on our future. Wrong turns can lead to long-term suffering, while the right ones result in a joyful life.

Isaac's instruction to Jacob confirmed he was disappointed by Esau's choice of his first two wives.

Often we tend to make more foolish choices because we don't want to admit we were wrong in the first place. Regardless of our stupidity, God is a God of second chances. If we are willing to change how we think and act, He forgives us and will *bless* us despite our past foolishness.

Make the wise choice of asking God's direction before you make any decision, and never stubbornly dig your heels in against His wisdom.

Choose wisely today.

My Turn

The little you had before I came has increased greatly, and the Lord has blessed you wherever I have been. But now, when may I do something for my own household?

Genesis 30:30

Everyone who works for a company knows their efforts, no matter how small, contribute to its success. The problem is we're often not recognized for our contributions. Employees who don't get the respect they feel they deserve will either cause trouble or quit.

Jacob worked for Laban, his father-in-law, for twenty years. He felt unappreciated, so he caused trouble and eventually quit. God had originally placed Jacob with Laban, but the time came for him to leave and make his own life.

God often places us where He wants us for a season but then leads us to move on to better places. Change can be scary, and it takes faith to move when we're in a safe, familiar place. We'll only know God's will by asking Him in prayer.

If your current situation is difficult, ask God if He wants you to change and how.

The comfort zone may not be where He wants us to be today.

AUGUST 4

Back to Basics

Worship the Lord your God, and his *blessings*
will be on your food and water.

Exodus 23:25

Food and water are the basic requirements of life.
We can live for about three weeks without food, but
only three days without water. In our society, if we need
food in our modern day we go grocery shopping, eat
out, or have our food delivered. For water, we only need
to turn on the tap.

In this verse, God is describing the Promised Land.
He promised that if the Israelites worshiped Him, He
would bless them by supplying all their needs. In His
kindness, God even provides food, water, and clothing
to those who don't love Him.

What He promises believers is much more.

Jesus said once we stop focusing on everything else
and start focusing on Him and helping others, we'll have
all we need here on Earth, and even more in Heaven.

Let's get back to those basics today.

Out of Control

As Jesus was saying these things, a woman in the crowd called out, *"Blessed* is the mother who gave you birth and nursed you."

Luke 11:27

We have no control over who our parents are and only some control over how our kids turn out. Parents try their best, but the results vary greatly. Bad parents often have good kids, and good parents frequently have bad kids. Regardless of a parent's successes and struggles, it is ultimately the children who must grow up and make their own choices; those choices determine their success or failure.

Here, Mary is being praised for being Jesus's mother, but in another verse, Jesus said, "Whoever does the will of my Father in Heaven is my brother and sister and mother."[52] He was reminding us that our earthly family is temporary, but our relationship with Him is permanent.

We can't control our past, but we can let God control our future.

Let Him do that today.

Knock-Out Punch

Then the man said, "Let me go, for it is day-break." But Jacob replied, "I will not let you go until you *bless* me."

Genesis 32:26

We won't always admit it, but many of us like a fight. The *Rocky* movies are still popular, and Olympic medals are awarded for boxing and wrestling. Whether it's fair or not, we also often root for the underdog to win.

Here, Jacob is the decided underdog: he was wrestling God, after all. As most good fathers would, God let him win. He was willing to challenge God in humility with boldness.

God likes to be challenged when we pray.

It has been said, "The prayer of a righteous man is powerful and effective." Let's put our full trust in God when we pray because we either believe He'll bless us or we don't.

Hope is getting into the ring. Faith is believing we'll win.

Challenge God in faith today.

Practice Makes Perfect

From the time he put him in charge of his household and all he owned, the Lord *blessed* the household of the Egyptian because of Joseph.

Genesis 39:5

Our jobs carry responsibilities: we have to do our work correctly and pay attention to all the details, and we must be sensitive to the people we work with, report to, or manage. Doing the little things right is the way we complete the "big picture."

Joseph's brothers sold him into slavery, where he earned the respect of a powerful Egyptian ruler and was put in charge of this man's estate. Through doing all the little things right, Joseph eventually became ruler of Egypt, second only to Pharaoh.

If we keep trusting God, keep a good attitude, and don't lose faith in Him, He will always take the bad situations we are faced with and use them to bless us. This is how He teaches us to have faith in Him regardless of our circumstances.

Like anything we do, the more we practice trusting God in every situation, the better we will get at it.

Practice trusting God today.

All in the Family

May God Almighty *bless* you and make you fruitful and increase your numbers until you become a community of peoples.

Genesis 28:3

Whether we come from a single-parent household, a home headed by a grandparent, a blended family, or a more traditional family, we all started out in a family. Whatever our family circumstances, God put us there to teach us the value of community. In a family, we learn that struggles, sharing, and dependence on those around us increase our love and understanding of others.

In this passage, Jacob's father is sending him away to find a wife. Isaac wasn't sure if he'd ever see his son again. He hoped Jacob's family would become a true community, depending on God and each other for support.

That should be our prayer for the members of our family, too. Distance, disagreements, and mixed memories can get in the way of community, especially between adult siblings.

Reaching out in forgiveness and love is the only path back to a united family.

Take that path today.

Bad Day

Cursed be the day I was born! May the day my mother bore me not be *blessed!*

Jeremiah 20:14

Depression isn't a modern illness: it's as old as mankind. Melancholy, "the blues," and suicide aren't new, either. The Bible records many suicides, from King Saul, Israel's first king, to Judas, who hung himself after he betrayed Jesus.

People don't commit suicide because they want to die but because they see no reason to continue living.

But there is always a reason for living, many just can't see it. The Bible tells us the devil has blinded the eyes of unbelievers so that they can't see the light of the Gospel of Jesus.[53] God's word is filled with life and promise if we would just read it.

Here Jeremiah is crying out in his depression. He was shunned, abused, and threatened for carrying God's warning message to His people. The people never responded to Jeremiah's message, which made him feel abandoned by God, too. Regardless, he always praised God and acknowledged that despite his misery, God was always with him.

We have it a lot easier than Jeremiah. God is always with us, even when we're having a bad day.

Remember that a bad day isn't a bad life, and soon, today will be a new tomorrow.

Superman

But his bow remained steady, his arms stayed limber, because of the hand of the Mighty One of Jacob, because of the Shepherd, the Rock of Israel, because of your father's God who helps you, because of the Almighty, who *blesses* you with the blessings of the skies above, blessings of the deep springs below, *blessings of the* breast and womb.

Genesis 49:24-25

Superman has always been a popular action hero because he's noble, honest, and has amazing strength. Many of the people God chose developed the same qualities, but most didn't have these qualities before God chose them.

God doesn't usually break the laws of physics for us, but He does give us supernatural power to overcome any obstacles in our path to serving Him.

According to His power that is at work within us, God is able to do more than we can ask or imagine.[54]

Imagine you are Superman (or Superwoman) today.

Fortune Telling

But Laban said to him, "If I have found favor in your eyes, please stay. I have learned from divination that the Lord has *blessed* me because of you."

Genesis 30:27

We'd all like to know what the future hold for us, wouldn't we? Many people use experts to help determine the future trends of financial markets, and one in seven Americans turn to fortune-tellers or astrologers to try to glimpse tomorrow. Yet the question remains: if any of these fortune-tellers could actually "see" the future, wouldn't they be wildly wealthy already?

Here, Jacob's father-in-law, Laban, used evil divination, only to learn he was blessed because of righteous Jacob. When Laban realized this, he tried to persuade Jacob not to move back to his homeland, despite how badly he had treated him.

Jacob, predictably, did not stay.

No one knows the future except God, and He doesn't need tarot cards or horoscopes. God wants us to count on Him, He knows the plans He has for us, plans to prosper us and to give us hope for the future.[55]

God even said when we listen to the Holy Spirit, He will show us things to come.[56]

Trust God today, and He will take care of tomorrow, tomorrow.

Lost and Found

"They are the sons God has given me here,"
Joseph said to his father. Then Israel said,
'Bring them to me so I may *bless* them."

Genesis 48:9

The experience of seeing long-lost family or friends
is priceless. Family and class reunions are popular because everyone attending is related by DNA or shared
life experiences. At these events, we can relax and be
ourselves because we're less at risk of being judged; everyone is just happy to see each other again.

God had changed Jacob's name to Israel, and here he
was meeting the grandsons through Joseph for the first
time. Israel had thought Joseph, his long-lost son, was
dead, only to find out that not only was he alive, but he
was also a great ruler in Egypt.

Finding God again later in life is just like this: we'd
been drifting and lost, so being reunited with God is
pure joy, and He is just as joyful to have us back with
Him again. Jesus said there is rejoicing in Heaven when
we repent or turn from our evil ways.[57]

God is never lost, and He makes Himself easy to
find. Just look around for Him today.

High and Dry

I have received a command to *bless*; He has *blessed*, and I cannot change it.

Numbers 23:20

There are always things we wish we could change. Changing the past may include correcting career choices, bad financial decisions, or words spoken in anger. Changing the present isn't easy, and it's often frightening.

"A bad known is better than a good unknown" is a phrase that all too often describes the way we face our decisions.

Balaam was hired to curse Israel, but God would only let him *bless* them instead. Yet, when God wants to bless us, we often stand in His way. If we only listened, He would tell us how to redirect our lives toward Him so we don't regret our future choices.

If we trust Him, He'll lead us through our troubled times.

If we don't, we may be left high and dry.

The future starts today.

Homeland Affairs

Jacob said to Joseph, "God Almighty appeared to me at Luz in the land of Canaan, and there He *blessed* me and said to me, 'I am going to make you fruitful and will increase your numbers. I will make you a community of peoples, and I will give this land as an everlasting possession to your descendants after you.'"

Genesis 48:3-4

"Home" can be a dorm, an apartment, a condo, or a house. Robert Frost said, "Home is the place where, when you have to go there, they have to take you in."

Here, Jacob is remembering God's promise of a homeland. He promises us one too: Heaven. Like any home, you have to belong to the family to get in. Jesus said He'll knock: is He enough of a part of our family that we'd let Him in?

Listen for His knock today.

Run the Risk

Now King David was told, "The Lord has *blessed* the household of Obed-Edom and everything he has, because of the ark of God." So David went to bring up the ark of God from the house of Obed-Edom to the City of David with rejoicing.

2 Samuel 6:12

Routine is a way of shaping our daily activities; it helps us regulate our lives. But routine can be a drug that keeps us from experiencing the "risky" life God may want for us.

Here, when King David last tried to move the Ark, it ended in disaster. When he saw God's blessings on its caretaker, Obed-Edom, he tried again; he had faith. Acting on faith is *always* risky. Faith means more than an assurance of Heaven. It means breaking routines and reaching out to others. When we risk, we're rewarded—with even more faith.

Ready to take some risks for God today?

More of Less

May the Lord, the God of your ancestors, increase you a thousand times and *bless* you as He promised!

Deuteronomy 1:11

More seems better than less, and big numbers often impress us. Getting a raise means we can save or spend more, but sometimes less is better.

Weighing less is usually good. Golf is based on the lowest score, and if we value humility, being less consumed with ourselves is a goal we should always strive to achieve.

In this verse, Moses is preparing to die and saying goodbye to his people. He prayed God would grow the nation of Israel. This happened for a while, but sadly, it did not last.

When Israel grew, the Israelites forgot God, so He reduced their numbers significantly; in response, they returned to Him, albeit temporarily.

Sometimes God allows us to be "pruned," so we return to basics, meaning our relationship with Him. In this way, we learn God doesn't want a part of us, He wants our whole life.

Sometimes less teaches us how to have more.

How can less be more today?

Return Policy

This is what the Lord Almighty, the God of
Israel, says: "When I bring them back from
captivity, the people of the land of Judah and
in its towns will once again use these words:
'The Lord *bless* you, O righteous dwelling,
prosperous city, O sacred mountain.'"

Jeremiah 31:23

Sometimes we return an item because it is defective
and needs repairing. Sometimes, though, we return
things for no real reason at all. Many stores won't accept a return if too much time has passed.

In this verse, God had *blessed* Israel in the Promised
Land, but they had abandoned Him in return. As He
promised, God removed the Israelites from their homeland until they learned to appreciate His blessings. The
sad part is they were held captive for seventy years in a
foreign country before they returned home.

In the same way, we can be held captive by our sins
and selfishness, but God has made a way for us to return to Him. No matter how long we've been gone or
how broken and defective we are, Jesus is where we go
for repairs.

Jesus is *always* the solution—the door through
Whom we return to God.[58]

Share with others that we can all return to God today.

Yikes!

Blessed is the one who waits for and reaches
the end of 1,335 days.

Daniel 12:12

Dying isn't something people like to dwell on. We
learn about death as children when one of our pets dies,
but we tend to think of "the end" as a theory, not as a
reality. That allows us to put off contemplating what
happens after death as long as possible.

This is why churches are filled with older people;
they've learned to face the truth: no one gets out alive.

In this passage, the archangel Gabriel is telling Daniel about the number of days between events at the end
of the world.

Whether we face it or not, our time here is limited.
He's the path to life after death. His path is narrow, and
only a few will find it.

Choose His path, and follow Him today.

From Here to Eternity

May the Lord *bless* you from Zion, he who is
the Maker of heaven and earth.

Psalm 134:3

Our perspective on life changes as we age, and what
used to be important is replaced by other priorities.
While getting a promotion, driving a fast car, or having
a hot date are significant to younger people, health and
retirement funds are usually bigger issues later in life.

The Israelites' view of life changed dramatically and
often, but not because of their age. The nation went
from freedom to slavery and back again many times
over the centuries.

As a result, Israel sang this psalm requesting God's
blessing on their way to Jerusalem (Zion) for various
festivals. In this way, they focused on seeking God's
blessing as their priority.

Whatever the current situation, make seeking God
the priority and ask Him for His blessings. May He
bless us all from Zion, too.

We need it more than ever today.

Tree of Life

She is a tree of life to those who take hold of
her; those who hold her fast will be *blessed*.

Proverbs 3:18

Trees symbolize growth and stability. Adam and
Eve walked under the shade of The Tree of Life in the
Garden of Eden, and it reminded them of God's presence in their lives. It has been said, "The best time to
plant a tree was twenty years ago; the second best time
is today."

Here, Solomon compares wisdom to a Tree of Life.
We spend our lives pursuing money and material
things that vanish. Wisdom is the key to finding God,
which is the only thing that holds true value.

Later, Solomon says the fear of the Lord is the beginning of wisdom. This is sound advice we are to heed.

Let's stop planting things that will disappear and
start cultivating our relationship with God.

He is the true Tree of Life—the Vine from which our
life is sustained.

Let's cling to the new Tree of Life, Jesus, all day today.

Rocket Science

Whoever gives heed to instruction prospers,
and *blessed* is the one who trusts in the Lord.
Proverbs 16:20

We're not a society that likes to follow the leader. We like to do things "my way," as Frank Sinatra declared, and men, in particular, don't like asking directions or reading instructions. "We'll figure it out!" they say.

This independent approach stems in part from our frontier heritage; that attitude helped our ancestors overcome great odds to make a good life for themselves and, by extension, us.

Yet Solomon warns that reading the instructions is critical to prosperity and *blessing*. He is referring to the wisdom and guidance in God's operating manual, the Bible. God wants us to know how to succeed in this world and how to find the Way to the next.

The closer we follow His directions, the more we'll learn from Him and the more we'll trust Him.

It's not exactly rocket science!

All His instructions are in the Bible; read it today.

Even the Score

They will receive *blessing* from the Lord and vindication from God their Savior.

Psalm 24:5

It feels good to be proven right, especially if our integrity or reputation has been attacked wrongfully. If fixing the problem takes too long, we often harbor resentment and wait for an opportunity to even the score.

Here, David is praising those with pure hearts and clean hands. He is telling us God will defend and *bless* us if we walk in His way. Still, God is patient with us, and shouldn't we expect Him to behave the same way towards our enemies?

Remember, we've hurt others, too, and those we have wronged may want Him to pay us back for what we did to them.

Let's consider mercy for them, just as God has shown us mercy because, as it says in the Bible, blessed are the merciful, for they will be shown mercy.[59]

Pray He won't want to even the score with us today!

Hell or High Water

Blessed are those whose help is the God of Jacob, whose hope is in the Lord their God.

Psalm 146:5

It is a fact that we'll always need help throughout our life. Infants and the elderly need help with the simplest tasks. Young people need help navigating homework and puberty. Adults rely on others for everything from getting help at work, help at home, and help to maneuver through a complex life dominated by technology.

Hope means believing that things will improve and that the help we need will arrive in time.

People often disappoint us, but this psalm urges us to put our trust and hope in God; He never disappoints.

If we keep our hope in Him, we'll be rescued from the hell, as well as the high water, that life may dump on us today.

Life is Short

Behold, I come like a thief! *Blessed* is he who stays awake and keeps his clothes with him, so that he may not go naked and be shamelessly exposed.

Revelation 16:15

Security has become an obsession these days. We have passwords on our phones and chips in our credit cards. Fingerprint scanning is being replaced by facial recognition software, but ultimately, none of this is foolproof; we'll always be vulnerable.

That is unless we remain close to Jesus.

He said He'll come like a thief because He's going to arrive suddenly and when we least expect Him. Amazingly, this promise is our greatest security, but will we be ready to meet Him when it happens?

Our material security in this life is fleeting, but it's not hard to prepare for eternal security. All we have to do is accept Jesus as Savior and love His people who are all around us.

Remember today that life is short, but eternity isn't.

Culture Shock

May He give you and your descendants the *blessing* given to Abraham, so that you may take possession of the land where you now reside as a foreigner, the land God gave to Abraham.

Genesis 28:4

Immigrants from another country experience culture shock because things in the new one are so different. We experience culture shock when our new society doesn't seem to honor many of the virtues and traditions we cherish. Often, if we don't agree with the latest cause or crusade, we are labeled as "backwards" or "bigots."

Here, Isaac felt the same way and was asking God to bless his son, Jacob, and later bring him back to his homeland once he had found a wife. Both of these men knew they were waiting for the promise of owning the land, a promise that was only fulfilled over four hundred years after the initial promise to Abraham when their descendants were finally set free from being slaves in Egypt.

All Christians are foreigners in this world, which is why it sometimes seems that we don't belong. Ultimately, we have a Heavenly home to which we'll return.

The passport to Heaven is Jesus. Apply for Him today.

Shout It Out

He stood and *blessed* the whole assembly of Israel in a loud voice.

1 Kings 8:55

Shouting is a natural reaction to major events in our lives. It may be for joy over the birth of a child, or it may be in anger over an injustice done. It may even be a shout of encouragement to our favorite sports team.

Here, Solomon is dedicating God's temple, which stood for 410 years. He spoke in a loud voice because there were no microphones, but also, he wanted everyone to hear how good his God was.

These days we don't need a brick-and-mortar temple, Jesus will dwell inside us if we let Him. He's ready to rescue us, bless us, and give us peace. All we have to do is open the doors of our own temple.

The question is: are we willing to shout our gratitude, as well?

Yet, many times, even whispering God's goodness into someone's ear is as effective as shouting it out for all to hear.

However it's done, try to share Jesus with someone today.

Hearing Impaired

However, the Lord your God would not listen
to Balaam but turned the curse into a *blessing*
for you, because the Lord your God loves you.

Deuteronomy 23:5

There's a big difference between hearing and listening. We hear many things we really don't listen to; our ears hear, but our brain listens. When we focus on the message, we are listening. When we listen, we learn.

God refused to listen to Balaam's curse, but He listens closely to gratitude and praise. Like God, we must decide when to listen and when to ignore.

We need to ignore gossip and negative talk because it is so destructive and, as Solomon said, it separates close friends.[60]

In contrast, listening to God will teach us to be like Him.

Talk less about other people and more about God today.

The Gospel Truth

Jacob said to his father, "I am Esau your first born. I have done as you told me. Please sit up and eat some of the game, so that you may give me your *blessing*."

Genesis 27:19

Because God is Truth, He hates it when we lie. We try to soften our lies by disguising them with phrases like "telling a fib," "bending the truth," and "telling a white lie."

The fact is, these are lies, and when we don't tell the truth, one lie often needs another lie to cover it up.

Jacob deceived his father to steal his brother's *blessing*, and despite God honoring the legal agreement, Jacob suffered greatly for the way he went about it.

God always condemns falsehood.

It represents a denial of His truth and a lack of faith. The truth is the truth, no matter how uncomfortable it can make us feel.

Jesus said, "The truth will set you free."[61] If you always tell the truth, you'll never have to remember what you said.

Speak the truth in love and live in freedom today.

Second Chance

Who knows? He may turn and relent and leave behind a *blessing*—grain offerings and drink offerings for the Lord your God.

Joel 2:14

Life is a series of second chances. Babies fall and get up again; students fail tests and then make the grade; singles date, break up and give it another go.

God is a God of second chances, and He, too, wants us to keep trying. We sin continually, but because of our faith in His Son Jesus, God continues to have mercy on us. He loves us despite our faults.

His Word says if we confess our sins, He is faithful and just and will forgive us, purifying us from all unrighteousness.[62]

Pray and be thankful for a second—and a third, a fourth and a hundredth—chance today.

Shared Values

If I had seen anyone perishing for lack of clothing, or the needy without garments, and their hearts did not *bless* me for warming them with the fleece from my sheep...

Job 31: 19-20

Babies have many self-centered demands, but only because they can't do anything for themselves. Sadly, it seems many of us never grow out of that: we're naturally selfish and find it hard work to be generous and share with others. This is why parents have to teach children to share.

Here, Job is reminding his friends that he shares often. Do we? Sharing money is one thing; sharing our faith is something else. Jesus paid a very high price for our salvation. Shouldn't we take the time to share the difference He's made in our lives?

We have the answer to the world's pain and misery, but do we have the courage to share it?

Action will cure fear today.

Double Down

> You drive the women of my people from their
> pleasant homes. You take away my *blessing*
> from their children forever.
>
> **Micah 2:9**

The family unit is under great stress. Living together before getting married seems to have become
the rule, not the exception. Money, sexual issues, and
even envy among couples breeds tension that can crush
relationships.

Here, the prophet Micah is telling the Israelite men
the bitter truth. Their uncaring, selfish behavior fell
hardest on their women and children. Even today, men
often use money to control women, and women use
their children to control men.

God does not approve of this behavior at all.

He wants us to love and nurture our families, but if
we don't double down on that, then the prophecies in
chapter two of Micah's book may come true.

We don't want that to happen, so let's double down
on genuinely loving others today.

Work It Out

The Lord your God has *blessed* you in all the work of your hands.

Deuteronomy 2:7

Most jobs require our time, talent, and effort, but whether we like our work or not, we get paid to do it, so we should always do our best. This is because our employers and our families depend on our commitment.

In fact, guiding, loving, protecting, and providing for our families is the work God *blesses* the most.

In this passage, Moses acknowledges the pain the Israelites experienced during their forty years in the desert and pronounces a blessing on their work as a result. This shows God appreciates our commitment to our career and our family. He *blesses* our effort, not our results. Mother Teresa said, "We are called to be faithful, not successful."

Be faithful today.

Rest in Peace

The best of all your first fruits and all of your special gifts will belong to the priests. You are to give them the first portion of your ground meal so that a *blessing* may rest on your household.

Ezekiel 44:30

What matters most? Wealth, health, or family? We all have our priorities, and they differ as we age. Younger people are concerned about dates and mates, yet older adults feel that young folks worry about the wrong things.

Here, the lesson is simple: God reminds us that He should be our priority, that He deserves our undivided attention and focus. This is because when we prioritize our relationship with Him, all of our problems become smaller, and we can rest in Him.

Rest in His peace today.

Stuck Up

But now they call the arrogant *blessed*.

Malachi 3:15

Of all the negative human traits, arrogance is probably the most disliked because it shows total self-centeredness. Working around stuck up people makes us edgy and angry, but humble people, on the other hand, are typically well-liked. This is because humble personalities emphasize others' needs above their own; however, we're all stuck up in our own ways sometimes.

Throughout the Bible, God condemns arrogance, and this verse is an excellent example of this.

Here, Malachi is depicting a world turned upside down. The prophet describes a society where arrogance is being honored and even *blessed*.

Sound familiar?

Jesus is God, but He humbled Himself to become a servant to mankind. In these troubled modern times, our only hope is to follow Jesus's example.

Let's humble ourselves today before He has to humble us again.

Reservation Required

Then Esau said to his father, "Do you have only one *blessing*, my father. *Bless* me too, my father!" Then Esau wept aloud.

Genesis 27:38

Reservations are required for popular restaurants because the number of people wanting to dine there exceeds the amount of space available. Having a reservation assures us we'll be welcome upon arrival, but neglecting to reserve a table ahead of time can cause embarrassment, disappointment, and frustration.

In this verse, Jacob stole a *blessing* reserved for his twin brother. Esau had previously been a fool for selling his birthright to Jacob, probably thinking it wouldn't matter because the blessing from their father is what would count.

Jacob outwitted Esau again by stealing his *blessing*, as well.

God doesn't honor foolish behavior, but He always rewards wisdom. Jacob showed wisdom in desiring the family birthright and the blessing above all else. He didn't go about it the right way, but he was clearly shown more righteous than Esau, who sold his birthright for a bowl of stew.

How can we secure our reservation in Heaven today?

Breaking Point

For this is what the Lord says: "Do not enter a house where there is a funeral meal; do not go to mourn or show sympathy, because I have withdrawn My *blessing*, My love and My pity from this people," declares the Lord.

Jeremiah 16:5

We get plenty of do-overs during our lives. We screw up, fail and blow opportunities. Paul even compares us to earthen vessels, which means we're fragile, like pottery: we can crack and break at any time.

In this verse, God is at a breaking point with the Israelites because of their idolatry. We love to look back and condemn the Israelites, telling ourselves we would never worship idols. But is this true?

An idol is anything that is prioritized above God.

God is loving, amazingly patient, and kind...but it is a scary thing when God reaches His breaking point. It is only when we are diligent in putting God first in our lives, each and every day, that we are sure to escape this grave danger.

God doesn't want lip service. He wants us to surrender our lives to Him today.

Confidence Building

But *blessed* is the man who trusts in the Lord,
whose confidence is in Him.

Jeremiah 17:7

We all have confidence doing something we're good at, but we quickly lose it when we do something we're less comfortable with. There are endless books, podcasts, and classes designed to increase our confidence, but the strongest boost comes from our own experience and abilities. Unfortunately, this can sometimes lead to overconfidence, resulting in arrogance and pride.

Solomon told us pride can result in disgrace, but humility brings wisdom.[63]

In this passage, Jeremiah says we shouldn't trust in ourselves or other people but rather place our total confidence in God.

Faith is another word for confidence in God, but are we truly confident He loves us and is always active in our life?

It's easy to say, "In God We Trust," but how can that be lived out today?

Take Up the Challenge

Do not repay evil with evil or insult with insult. On the contrary, repay evil with *blessing*,
because to this you were called so that you
may inherit a *blessing*.

1 Peter 3:9

Evil and insults to our values are all around us; a
glance at the news or the internet will confirm this. Insults disrespect and taunt us, and in turn, tempt us to
become vengeful. We want to return the slight with a
bigger one, but should we?

Paul agrees with Peter's challenge in this verse and
reminds us that we should *bless* those who persecute
us.[64]

Peter and Paul's example came directly from Jesus,
Who was silent on the cross and never uttered a single
insult to His torturers.

That sort of reaction can only come from Jesus, Who
dwells in us and will give us the grace to do it, too.

Let's pray for peace and patience to take up every
challenge that we will face today.

Kingdom Come

May nations serve you and peoples bow down
to you. Be lord over your brothers, and may
the sons of your mother bow down to you.
May those who curse you be cursed and those
you *bless* be *blessed*.

Genesis 27:29

It's fun to dream of being a king or queen, having
people bow and curtsy to us. We would have a kingdom
and power and live in a castle protected by knights in
armor. The reality is we don't live in a castle, but as His
disciples, Jesus has given us power, authority, and access to His Kingdom.

Isaac is *blessing* Jacob in this verse and predicting
great things that only God could bring about. Yet God
would humble Jacob before His blessing was fulfilled.

In the same way, He may humble us so that we are
equipped for the blessing He has in store for us. Remember, Jesus, our King, came to serve, not be served.
True nobility is serving others and putting them first.

Jesus said the last will be first,[65] so let's head to the
back of the line today.

SEPTEMBER 9

Peace and Quiet

When David returned home to *bless* his household, Michel daughter of Saul came out to meet him and said, "How the king of Israel has distinguished himself today, going around half-naked in full view of the slave girls of his servants as any vulgar fellow would!"

2 Samuel 6:20

Home isn't always sweet. Spouses can be stressful, and children can be frustrating and loud. Sometimes, even loneliness, sickness, and addiction can be found there.

David's marriage to Michel was strained. She tried to shame him and humiliate him, but it didn't work. He was celebrating before God, and he knew he was right.

Trying to control our family never works out, yet leading them in the ways of God always pays off in the end. His peace surpasses all understanding, so pray for and practice peace—not just in the world, but in the world within the four walls of the home.

He wants us to experience His peace. Pray for that, and a little quietness, today.

Happy Ending

Blessed are those who hear it and take to heart what is written in it, because the time is near.
Revelation 1:3

Did you know computer algorithms can forecast human actions? They're used to predict the stock market and to create self-driving cars. But what does God say about the future?

In this verse from Revelation, Jesus is saying that mankind will lose its quest for self-perfection, and the world will collapse into evil and be destroyed.

Only God's children will be saved.

It is a happy ending for some, but maybe not the way we would write the story. Whether "near" means today or a thousand years from now, being ready means we're obeying His commands of loving Him and our neighbors daily.

Live today as if the time is near.

SEPTEMBER 11

Uncertain Future

The Lord *blessed* the latter part of Job's life
more than the first.

Job 42:12

Delayed gratification is nice in theory, and saving
for the future is wise, provided we live to enjoy it. In
Jesus's story of the rich fool, the man retired with his
wealth but died that very night.[66] We all know of good,
younger people who die, and eventually, we all die.

The bottom line is that tomorrow is not guaranteed.

Job is a classic example of uncertainty. He was an
extraordinarily wealthy and healthy man who loved
God and had a great family. It was all taken from him
in a matter of days, without warning. While Job blamed
God for his situation, he didn't doubt Him. He knew
God would ultimately rescue him, whether on Earth or
in Heaven.

The fact that he was eventually *blessed* here on Earth
is a nice ending and a testament to God's merciful nature, but it doesn't always happen that way.

Where and how our ending will be written, God only
knows.

Pray to be ready if it happens today.

Give and Take

Blessed are those who have regard for the weak;
the Lord delivers him in times of trouble.

Psalm 41:1

Our views of charity may differ, but charity is an attempt to share with others. A number of people volunteer their time and service in an attempt to make a difference; others give money. Some, however, believe that if you help too much, you enable dependency.

Yet studies show that those of more modest means donate a greater percentage of their income to charity than the ultra-wealthy. Perhaps it's because they've benefited from charity before. Perhaps they know "need" firsthand.

While all of our intentions may be noble, serving and sharing are two of the few visible signs of our Christian love.

Give time and resource, and take His blessings today.

SEPTEMBER 13

Eye to Eye

But *blessed* are your eyes because they see, and
your ears because they hear.

Matthew 13:16

Events have taken place in the past that most of us
would love to see firsthand: the moment our parents
met, for instance. History buffs would be thrilled to
watch the Gettysburg Address, see the Wright Brothers
fly, or observe the D-Day invasion.

We long for past glory days, and while we wish we
could see into the future, we're trapped in the present.

In this verse, Jesus is telling His disciples how fortunate they are to be with Him in the flesh. Many kings,
people, and prophets wanted to see the fulfillment of
the Messiah's coming but didn't get the chance. Thank
God He's still with us, and we can go to Him anytime.

What can we do today to move beyond the past and
begin to prepare for the future with Him?

Straight Ahead

Blessed is the man who makes the Lord his trust, who does not look to the proud, to those who turn aside to false gods.

Psalm 40:4

These days, we're distracted by phone calls, text messages, and emails. In fact, a major purpose of advertising is to disturb our focus so that we only pay attention to the ads. As a result, it becomes so easy for our attention to be turned to the false gods of appearance, status, and possessions.

This verse warns us not to chase after things or people but to focus on God instead. Idolizing anything else leads to envy, frustration, and sin. A person's character was once the measure of their greatness; now, we seem to measure greatness in terms of net worth or degrees of fame.

Jesus lived simply, and He wants us to live simply, too, with our eyes focused straight ahead on His call.

Distracted driving can be fatal; so can distracted living.

Concentrate on following Him today.

Circle the Wagons

For surely, O Lord, you *bless* the righteous;
you surround them with Your favor as with
a shield.

Psalm 5:12

When pioneers went west in wagon trains, they were often attacked by Native Americans. Quickly, they realized that if they formed their wagons into a circle, they could more easily defend themselves.

This psalm reminds us that God is our shield and defender. That doesn't mean we'll never be attacked; it means when we are, God has promised He is with us, and He supports us. Sometimes, He even lets things severely challenge us in order to grow our character.

That's when we need to lean on Him the most and grow the relationship.

Whether we ever see a victory doesn't matter; only our faith, patience, and hope in Him, today, do.

WrestleMania

Jacob said, "Please tell me your name." But He replied, "Why do you ask my name?" And He *blessed* him there.

Genesis 32:29

Many high schools and colleges have successful wrestling programs. It is a sport of strength, agility, and balance, and as any wrestler knows, it is also exhausting.

In this scripture, Jacob wrestled with God all night and never gave up. God *blessed* him because Jacob believed God had the power to *bless* him. Unlike Jacob, who wrestled with God, Paul says we now must wrestle against powers of darkness, but God has supplied all the armor and weapons we will need to win.[67]

Jacob's fight ended at the light of dawn. Jesus is our light. Focus on His power when wrestling with life today.

Some Will, Some Won't

> Then Jacob *blessed* Pharaoh and went out from his presence.
> **Genesis 47:10**

We often want God to *bless* only those who follow Him, yet we know that just as the rain falls on crops and weeds alike, God's *blessings* fall on everyone. The financially successful, the rich and famous, and the folks who live long, healthy lives may or may not believe in God; there is no question, however, that they have been *blessed*.

Like Job, Jeremiah, and Habakkuk, we struggle with this.

In this verse, Jacob is *blessing* the Egyptian Pharaoh, who worshiped the sun god, but we have to remember being *blessed* isn't the same as being saved. In a parable that Jesus told, a farmer ordered his harvesters not to pull the weeds out of the wheat field in order to protect against the wheat being pulled out by mistake.[68] Rather, He said, they will be sorted at harvest time.

This means everyone will get their due in God's time, so let's never be envious of anyone else's *blessings*, let's be thankful for the *blessings* we receive.

Everyone may be *blessed*, and that's the goodness of God. When it comes to spending eternity with God, though, we will all have made our choice before we stand before Him. Some will spend eternity with Him, and some won't.

Eternity starts today. Get going!

Charmed Life

From this day on I will *bless* you.

Haggai 2:19

How would we act if we knew that from this day on, we'd be *blessed*? Hopefully, we'd be excited about the future and less fearful about sharing our true feelings. We'd also be braver in making life decisions because we'd be more optimistic. We'd be bolder in sharing our faith, as well, because rejection wouldn't mean that much to us.

The Israelites had been oppressed and living in spiritual and material poverty for many years, but in Haggai's prophecy, that's exactly what God promised the Israelites, blessings from that day forward. They believed that and quickly acted in obedience by starting to rebuild the temple.

God has made the same promise to us: from this day on, He will *bless* us.

Believing that promise is the only secret to living a charmed life. Start really believing today.

Test Case

"Bring the whole tithe into the storehouse, that there may be food in my house. Test Me on this," says the Lord Almighty, "and see if I will not throw open the floodgates of heaven and pour out so much *blessing* that you will not have room enough for it."

Malachi 3:10

Our faith is not what we were born into or what was passed down to us. Some say, "I'm a Baptist," or "a Methodist," or "a Catholic," but most "fill-in-the-blank" Christians have never truly been tested on whether God's promises are true.

We need to have our own authentic relationship with God, not an inherited religion.

In Malachi, God is angry because the Israelites merely filled in the blank with "Israelite." Their faith was on paper, not in their heart. God wants to be tested on His promises; that's how we discover He's not a paper god, but the One, true God, Who loves us and rewards our obedience.

Are we willing to test our faith in God today?

Underdogs

> As you have been an object of cursing among
> the nations, O Judah and Israel, so will I save
> you, and you will be a *blessing*. Do not be
> afraid, but let your hands be strong.
>
> **Zechariah 8:13**

We all like to root for underdogs, the person or team that makes a great comeback, overcoming huge obstacles to win against tremendous odds. We like these stories because, unfortunately, they are pretty rare. Most of the time, the big, strong, and powerful win.

Thankfully, that's not how God works.

In this verse, the Israelites have returned from exile to find their country in ruins. God, however, wasn't done with them, and He promised to restore their nation. Paul pointed out that God chooses the weak to shame the strong.[69] The Israelites knew who won the victory, and it wasn't them!

Through Jesus, we have our success, and He deserves our thanks and praise.

God gets His work done through underdogs, not show dogs.

Who will we give credit to for our victories today?

Comfort Zone

Blessed are those who mourn, for they will be comforted.

Matthew 5:4

Mourning is the emotion we want to avoid most. Mourning the deaths of family members or close friends is terribly painful, and only the passing of time brings us any relief. It can feel like waves of grief pounding the heart; eventually, the waves tend to fade over time, though they can randomly crash over us out of the blue, even years later.

Jesus tells us in this verse that we'll be comforted in our mourning by trusting Him. This is because mourning should make people turn to God for support and solace. For those who believe, we know that our close ones who die in Him will be in Heaven, and that we'll be following them at some point.

In mourning, we can be comforted because Heaven is filled with joy.

Losing someone close to us on Earth is our loss, not theirs.

Is there someone in mourning that we can comfort today?

Rescue Adoption

Then he *blessed* Joseph and said, "May the God before whom my fathers Abraham and Isaac walked, the God who has been my shepherd all my life to this day, the Angel who delivered me from all harm—may He *bless* these boys. May they be called by my name and the names of my fathers Abraham and Isaac, and may they greatly increase on the earth."

Genesis 48:15-16

When an adopted child is taken into a new home, they become heirs of that family. The child becomes a full member of the family, with all the love and legal rights due to every other member.

In this verse, Jacob is adopting his son Joseph's children into his family. That is what God does when we accept Jesus as our Savior. We're rescues from our old, sinful life, and we become His children.

We're not guests or employees; we're family members.

Who can we help rescue today?

Good News, Bad News

Now when Balaam saw that it pleased the Lord to *bless* Israel, he did not resort to divination as at other times, but he turned his face toward the wilderness.

Numbers 24:1

Someone once said, "The bad news is that nothing lasts forever; the good news is that nothing lasts forever."

The bad news is that Balaam was asked to curse the people of Israel. The good news for Israel is that God would only let Balaam *bless* them.

Jesus also gave us the good news that He would save us from our sins if we believe in Him. The bad news, of course, is if we don't believe and trust in Him, we choose not to be saved.

More good news is that Jesus still seeks out those who are lost, continually giving them the chance to come to Him.

Always choose Jesus's good news over the bad news of the world.

Jesus said, "Take Heart! I have overcome the world."[70] Share that news today.

On the Level

What are you, O mighty mountain? Before
Zerubbabel you will become level ground.
Then he will bring out the capstone with
shouts of "God *bless* it! God *bless* it!"

Zechariah 4:7

A snow-capped mountain can look imposing. Like
the vastness of an immovable mountain, our concerns
and problems are often overwhelming, and they can
seem slick and impossible to get over.

The Israelites' continued lack of faith and their at-
tachment to the ungodly cultures of the neighboring
peoples made the idea of rebuilding God's temple almost impossible.

It became Israel's self-made mountain.

Yet God used Zerubbabel to start the seemingly impossible job and then to finish it. He did. God has also
given us a job to do.[71] We need to search that purpose
out and then do it. He will help us overcome that mountain, and when we do, we'll be standing on His level
ground.

Everything is possible today for one who believes.[72]

Standard of Living

"Then all the nations will call you *blessed*, for yours will be a delightful land," says the Lord Almighty.

Malachi 3:12

We never get tired of being recognized for our contributions or praised for our accomplishments. Sometimes, the credit may not actually belong to us completely, and if we're honest, we'll admit we don't really deserve all the attention.

Here, God isn't praising the Israelites. He's telling them about the blessings He's prepared for them if they make an effort in being generous toward Him and others. Thankfully, God *blesses* us even when we're undeserving of His kindness.

By acknowledging Jesus as our Savior, we're now His children, and He loves us. It's difficult to live up to His high standards, yet when we surrender to God's grace, He'll *bless* our effort.

When we give control to God, others will notice the blessing on our life.

Make the effort today.

Seeing is Believing

Then He turned to His disciples and said pri-
vately, "*Blessed* are the eyes that see what you
see."

Luke 10:23

We've all said, "I'll believe it when I see it," but we
believe in lots of things without seeing them: atoms,
places we've never been, and historical events we've
read about. The idea that we believe what we see can be
deceptive. Modern technologies like virtual reality and
computer-generated imagery make things that don't
exist seem amazingly real.

In this verse, Jesus reminds His disciples of the
extraordinary privilege they had in sharing the time
in history with Him and seeing His miracles. Watching Jesus heal the blind, deaf, mute, and disabled must
have been overwhelming and awe-inspiring.

Today we believe by faith. We believe because we
know He is God, and God is not limited by time and
space: He created those, along with everything else.

God is constantly working miracles. Look for those
today.

Welcome Back

After Jacob returned from Paddan Aram, God appeared to him again and *blessed* him.

Genesis 35:9

Vietnam veterans came home to a country that had changed dramatically. Those of us who move away from the place we grew up have similar experiences when we go "home."

In this verse, Jacob returned home after spending twenty years in a foreign country. When he left, he was single, his brother hated him, and both of his parents were living. By the time he returned, though, he had twelve sons by four women, he and his brother had reconciled, and though his mother had passed away, he managed to make it back while his father was still alive.

No matter how old we are, God isn't done with us, either. We don't know what's going to happen in the next twenty years (or, for that matter, in the next twenty minutes). God protected Jacob while he was gone, and He will protect us while we're here. God wants us to embrace change, not hide from it. If we have faith like Jacob, He will bless whatever those changes are.

Our circumstances will change; God won't.

Let's embrace the change God wants in us today.

Security Risk

Blessed are the peacemakers, for they will be called sons of God.

Matthew 5:9

Peacemakers are sometimes seen as "wimpy" because some want peace at any price. While being a peacemaker is generally a good thing, being a pushover wasn't exactly what Jesus meant when He gave His Sermon on the Mount. Christians have to stand up for their place in society and culture.

But are we going to be radical followers of Christ, or are we going to shrink into a holy huddle?

One reason we might shrink back is that many people picture Christians as judgmental, not peacemaking. Yet our Leader died for our sins, not His. He has no illusions that we are better than anyone else; He just wanted us to be His ambassadors, spreading peace everywhere.

This isn't a security risk involving a leak of top-secret information; it's in the gospels, and it's called God's salvation plan.

How can we be ambassadors of the gospel of peace today?

Ancient History

> After spending some time there, they were
> sent off by the believers with the *blessing* of
> peace to return to those who had sent them.
>
> **Acts 15:33**

This passage was a pivotal point in Christian history. There was a huge debate as to whether "Gentiles," or non-Jews, should be required to follow Jewish traditions like dietary rules or circumcision.

This debate came to a head when Paul and Barnabas returned to Jerusalem with reports of the tremendous acceptance of the Gospel by the Gentiles. The Church elders agreed with Paul and Barnabas and decided that the Gentiles did not have to follow most of the Jewish traditions, and they sent men to Antioch to explain their decision.

Two thousand years later, we're the products of that decision.

Think carefully and wisely about all of the decisions to be made today.

Fall Forward

Blessed is anyone who does not stumble on account of me.

Matthew 11:6

Amazing performances happen in professional sports. Whether it's catching a line drive up the middle, snagging the football just inside the goal line, or sinking a twenty-foot putt, professional sports are frequently about making the near-impossible seem easy.

The truth is that many, many dropped balls, interceptions, and bad swings happened along the way. The difference is those stumbles usually occurred without an audience.

In this verse, Jesus is warning against stumbling. It's easy to fake being Christian; we can talk about the Bible, go to church, and attend small groups, all while still having unbelieving hearts. Whether we're a social or business predator, it's all the same. It's about *"my"* self-gratification.

Jesus knows we will trip. Pray He'll be there to catch us all day today.

Pay Back

But when you give a banquet, invite the poor, the crippled, the lame, the blind and you will be *blessed*. Although they cannot repay you, you will be repaid at the resurrection of the righteous.

Luke 14:13-14

Many of us wouldn't invite homeless people into our homes for a party. We have convinced ourselves their behavior would be inappropriate, they would smell bad, and they would probably be drunk.

But in this verse, Jesus is commanding us to open our doors.

He clearly tells us to serve others, including the poor and homeless. Jesus always rebukes those who have much but give little. "Pay it forward" implies someone has to repay us, but God doesn't owe us anything. "Pay it back" is more accurate because God has provided all we have. We can never hope to pay His *blessings* back, but by helping the hopeless here, we can do *something* and store up treasure in Heaven, as well.

Who needs our help today?

Dig In

Look, I am coming soon! *Blessed* is he who keeps the words of the prophesy written in this scroll.

Revelation 22:7

Are we waiting for an engraved invitation? People who search for meaning without seeking God are chasing the wind, but we don't need a net, a hook, or a trap to find Him. We just need to read the Bible and do what He says. He has revealed Himself through many prophets, miracles, and revelations.

The Bible is an instruction book for discovering who God is, what He wants from us, and how we are to act. He didn't write it in code; He made it plain to both the simple and the educated.

We will never find our way to true happiness until we open His book and read it. There are many pearls of wisdom to guide our lives if we dig in.

Jesus said if we seek, we'll find, and God's word has all the answers.

Dig in deep today.

Aging Out

Then Joseph brought his father Jacob in and presented him to Pharaoh. After Jacob *blessed* Pharaoh, Pharaoh asked him, "How old are you?"

Genesis 47:7

As we age, our attitude towards aging changes, too. Kids, in their excitement to get older, often round up their age and always look forward to their next birthday. Young adults can't wait to be old enough to drive or drink legally. Rounding down starts around the age of fifty, when birthdays become more painful.

But we're all getting older and closer to death.

Before we reach that final day, we have two choices: the world's way or God's way. The world's way treats death as a theory, not a reality. There may be life after death, but we'll deal with that much later. God's way includes plenty of enjoyment, but also the certainty that we'll have to account for our lives, starting with our relationship with Jesus.

It's not life after death we should fear. It's death after death, a hard thought for today—or any day.

Flesh and Blood

Jesus replied, "*Blessed* are you Simon, son of Jonah, for this was not revealed to you by flesh and blood, but by My Father in Heaven."
Matthew 16:17

In this scripture, Peter had just told Jesus that he believed that Jesus is the Son of God. Jesus Himself said, "I and the Father are One."[73] The author C.S. Lewis said, "He's either a lunatic, a liar or Lord."

Nothing else Jesus said or did displayed any possible mental imbalance at all. In fact, He consistently outwitted the smartest people of the time. So we can conclude He clearly wasn't a lunatic.

In His entire life, Jesus upset people with His openness, but He never once lied. So we can conclude He can't be called a liar.

The people who lived and walked with Jesus worshiped Him and called Him Lord. Many of them gave up their lives for this belief. No one gives up their life for a liar or a lunatic.

History shows the effect of Jesus's life on thousands upon thousands of people within a few decades after He left the Earth. Lies die out and are forgotten; the truth is undeniable. The truth of Jesus's Lordship is believed by billions of people around the world today.

How can we share this truth with those around us today?

True or False

He did not recognize him, for his hands were hairy like those of his brother Esau; so he proceeded to *bless* him.

Genesis 27:23

We all know lying is wrong, but it's often easy and sometimes useful. Sometimes, even flattery or being overly complimentary can cross the line between true and false.

Outright deception is the final outcome of small lies building into bigger ones. Jacob lied to his father by impersonating his brother. He stole his brother's *blessing* and left a centuries-long conflict between their descendants in his wake.

One lie leads to another, and little lies lead to big lies.

Jacob's lie shows that deception can lead to fractured relationships and a loss of trust. Is it ever worth it?

People who always tell the truth never have to remember what they said.

Tell the truth today.

OCTOBER 6

Perfect!

Therefore the Lord *blessed* the Sabbath day
and made it holy.

Exodus 20:11

Leisure and recreation all started with the Sabbath.
While life sometimes appears to have been simpler in
Biblical times, it was thoroughly unpredictable, and the
work was very hard.

Knowing all this, God tells the Israelites to stop all
work once a week to rest. But it wasn't just a holiday;
it was a day of connecting with God and family. Could
they really believe God would provide for them if they
took fifty-two days off from work each year? He certainly did, and He will for us, too.

Yet, we live in a society where vacation days go un-
used, and our children are raised by strangers.

Will God *bless* us if we spend more time with Him?
Yes, but remember quantity time doesn't equate to
quality time. Matthew tells us Jesus didn't perform
many miracles among His family and friends in Nazareth because of their lack of faith.

Can we really rest in the Lord today?

OCTOBER 7

The Right Place

> Wherever I cause My Name to be honored, I will come to you and *bless* you.
>
> **Exodus 20:24**

Places have a lot of meaning to us: childhood memories of playgrounds, backyards, beaches, and amusement parks always warm our hearts. On the other hand, the site of a tragedy, like the World Trade Center, is darker emotionally.

Places have meaning with God, too. That is because certain places remind us of God's relationship with us. He's always with us wherever we go, but we sometimes go to churches, mountains, forests, or other places of worship to find a physical connection with our God.

Jerusalem is the city where He put His Name, and it is still the Holy City. Whether we go there or some other place we choose, God wants us to seek Him and find Him. His word tells us we'll find Him when we seek Him with all of our heart.[74]

Where can we go today to find Him?

Wide Open

Those who went ahead and those who followed shouted, "Hosanna! *Blessed* is He who comes in the name of the Lord."

Mark 11:9

The media tries to get our attention continually. Sifting through the cries and shouts to determine what is real and what is not can be difficult. What is not difficult, though, is deciding what is real about Jesus's calls for our attention.

In this verse, Jesus came into Jerusalem as a hero. Some were convinced He was the Messiah. Others thought He was just a good man, but not the Christ. The religious leaders believed He was a rebel, stirring up the people.

Many people today believe Jesus was just a good man. Fewer believe He is God. Christianity is under attack more and more these days; Jesus predicted this, saying the path to destruction is wide, and the one to salvation is narrow.[75]

Which is the best road to follow today: the way of popular culture, or the Prince of Peace?

Calculated Risk

For I tell you, you will not see me again until you say, "*Blessed* is He who comes in the name of the Lord."

Matthew 23:39

Jesus told His disciples that He was going away, but He also said He would return. Either they didn't understand what He was saying, or they didn't want to and hoped it wouldn't happen.

Many of us are just like them: we don't take Jesus seriously. We read the Bible and can attend countless sermons and read an endless amount of books, but unless we experience God directly, it's just a story. The way we discover how to depend on God is by practicing our dependence on Him.

Risking ourselves for Him, even a little, helps us experience God's realness. He will help us overcome our fears, and we'll learn to trust Him instead of ourselves.

The risk isn't in trusting God, it's in *not* trusting Him. Take a calculated risk today with Him.

Mercy Me

Blessed are the merciful, for they will be shown mercy.

Matthew 5:7

We all think we deserve mercy, yet we want justice for those who have hurt us. We're all guilty of wrong-doings, whether they're little or big. The little ones are usually the result of stupidity or immaturity, and the bigger issues are the results of selfishness and spite. Spite is our deliberate attempt to harm someone, whether that is in an emotional sense or by smearing their reputation. We want to bring our brand of justice to bear. Revenge seems sweet.

We should focus less on demanding justice and instead pray for mercy. If God were to give us what we really deserve, our punishment would be eternally unbearable. Thankfully, because Jesus took our punishment, God is merciful and forgiving towards us. When will we start being merciful toward others?

If we treat others how we want to be treated, wouldn't we show them mercy instead of demanding justice?

Let's start being merciful today.

Game of Life

> Then he said, "Please my son, bring me some
> of your game to eat, so that I may give you my
> *blessing."*
>
> **Genesis 27:25**

As kids, we played board games, card games, and musical chairs. Games teach kids about winning, losing, sportsmanship, and acquiring skills. In fact, wild meat is called "game" because of the skill-set needed in hunting.

In this verse, two games are on display. Esau went to get game to serve to his father so he would receive his *blessing*, while Jacob played a far more serious game that involved deception.

We crave relationships where we can be real without gamesmanship, but those are rare. Thankfully, God doesn't play games; He plays for real, and He wants us to be real with others. Game playing is manipulation, and no one wins. In the game of life, play fair, play hard, and play real. We'll win some and lose some, but we'll never lose God's love for us.

God has already won the victory, and we are winners with Him.

Start acting like a winner today.

OCTOBER 12

Kid's Stuff

And He took the children in His arms, placed
His hands on them and *blessed* them.

Mark 10:16

Why do we love children so much? Being so cute is
one reason for sure. They also have unlimited energy,
and they love to play. Everything is new and full of wonder to kids, and that reminds us to appreciate the little
things in life more often. They also love unconditionally
and don't seem to notice when we're out of breath or
ready to surrender.

Jesus loves children because they have a simple faith
that is lacking in adults. They're innocent, and they
believe what they hear is the truth. They haven't been
dulled by betrayal or lies; skepticism hasn't taken hold.

Jesus wants us to have that level of faith in Him because He will never betray or lie to us.

Children trust their parents without question.

Believe, trust, love, and live like a child today.

Twelve Pack

All these are the twelve tribes of Israel, and
this is what their father said to them when he
blessed them, giving each the *blessing* appropriate for him.

Genesis 49:28

Thomas Jefferson correctly wrote that "all men are
created equal," but we're also all created *differently*. This
is best seen in families. Any family with more than one
child sees clear evidence of the great divide in personalities and temperaments.

Jacob's family was a total mess. He had twelve sons
by four different women. For several of his sons, Jacob's
blessing seemed a veiled curse. None of them were perfect, and neither are we. Our imperfections lead us to
Christ because He has a special love for misfits and sinners, just like us and our kids.

Thankfully, He didn't come to save perfect people;
He came to save us.

God sent Jesus to save us now, today![76]

Love-Hate Relationship

May those who pass by not say to them, "The *blessing* of the Lord be on you; we *bless* you in the name of the Lord."

Psalm 129:8

We're living in an imperfect world, and sadly, some people of other cultures seek to destroy our way of life. Why they hate us is a matter of debate: is it our freedom, or the way we rudely display it? It may be that the spread of our culture is seen as a threat to others.

The psalmist in this verse remembers how he was oppressed and tortured for his faith. The Lord rescued him, but he remains bitter. Many of us can also remember being belittled and bullied and how resentful it made us.

The psalmist wants the Lord to punish his persecutors and never bless them. Jesus would disagree with his request, but He does promise to avenge us.[77]

Trust only in God to make things right today.

Go With the Flow

Again the high priest asked Him, "Are You the Messiah, the Son of the *blessed* One?"

Mark 14:61

Jesus's reputation had swept through the countryside. He was performing miracles, challenging man-made authority, and drawing huge crowds. Jesus wasn't playing by the religious rules; He was preaching authentic living instead of the phony holiness of the leaders. He exposed their deception and hypocrisy, and they hated Him for it.

Jesus was tortured and crucified for rejecting their two-facedness. Outside of our holy bubble is a society that increasingly belittles and rejects Christ and Christianity. We are an irritating reminder of sin. Intolerance is a word sometimes used today to indicate a refusal to follow society's defiant disobedience to God.

Today will we stand with Jesus when challenged, or go with the flow?

Separation Anxiety

Then the King will say to those on His right,
"Come, you who are *blessed* by My Father; take
your inheritance, the kingdom prepared for
you since the creation of the world."

Matthew 25:34

Many people believe they're going to Heaven because they're a good person. Others believe there are many ways to get into Heaven. There is only one unbreakable rule to get into Heaven, however: confess Jesus as Savior, and believe that God raised Him from the dead.[78]

This verse emphasizes taking care of others. The scene is the end of the world; Jesus separates those who have been kind to the "least" from those who haven't. Those who were kind go to Heaven, and the others go to hell.

So how are we kind to the least? Jesus said when we feed the hungry and give them something to drink, we care for the least. When we invite strangers to join us, we are feeding and inviting Him.

Look for the least and try to bless them today.

Heart to Heart

Blessed are the pure in heart, for they will see God.

Matthew 5:8

Don't you wish following God was easier? This verse is showing us the surest path to seeing Him. Being pure in heart means having good motives, innocent actions, avoiding impure images, and, of course, the most challenging—being humble.

Jesus doesn't cut us any slack on this one. He knows we're going to be much more forgiving of ourselves than other people, so He sets the bar high to help us achieve big goals, like the purity of heart.

Notice He doesn't say "purity of actions."

If our heart is in the right place, our motives, actions, thoughts, and words will be pure, too. We may fail, but striving for purity while constantly trying to love others around us is the essence of a pure heart.

This is what Jesus calls for.

How can we avoid everything that threatens our purity today?

Marriage Made in Heaven

> Then the angel said to me, "Write this: '*Blessed* are those who are invited to the wedding supper of the Lamb!' And he added, 'These are the true words of God.'"

Revelation 19:9

Weddings are joyful and fun. Who doesn't like a party? Only certain people get invited, though, and brides-to-be often struggle over who should receive an invitation.

The Bible describes Heaven as a wedding feast where Jesus is marrying the Church. Like any wedding, God only invites those He knows. After all, we wouldn't ask strangers to attend our wedding, would we? Jesus said only those who do the will of God can enter His kingdom.[79]

To the rest, He will say, "I never knew you."

Doing God's will is simple: we need to accept Jesus as our Savior and love others. Those two straightforward actions will open the doors and usher us into the eternal presence of God.

How can we do God's will today?

Scaredy-Cat

But even if you should suffer for what is right, you are *blessed*. Do not fear their threats; do not be frightened.

1 Peter 3:14

Being a scaredy-cat means we're afraid when others aren't, but we're all frightened of some things that don't scare others. Younger people can't relate to the elderly's fear of falling, and middle-aged adults worry about careers and families, fears older folks have outgrown, and youngsters haven't yet considered.

Peter says, "Don't be afraid of anything, especially when we're doing the right thing."

The thought of getting mocked or rejected for sharing God's word is scary, especially if it's by close friends and family. If we were less frightened, we'd share the gospel with others in boldness, and we'd see a big difference in our society. People do respond to the gospel, so let's buckle up, be brave and take the risks Jesus wants us to.

There's only One person to fear. How can we get more courage today?

"How To" Guide

Tell Aaron and his sons, "This is how you are
to *bless* the Israelites."

Numbers 6:23

Praying is our way of talking to God, yet to pray
truthfully, we have to believe God actually exists. Many
people don't, but still, send up prayers "just in case." We
sometimes praise and thank God, but too often, we're
just looking for His handout. Of course, He doesn't
mind our asking because He loves us, but like any Father, He gives us what's good for us, and that's not always what we want. Also, remember "no" is an answer,
too!

In this verse, the Israelites needed encouragement,
and Aaron's *blessing* in the verses that follow show the
depth of God's desire to *bless* and protect us physically,
emotionally, and spiritually.

Since we're always asking God for things, let's ask
Him to show us how to be more committed to our relationship with Him.

Do we believe God will answer our prayers or are
they "just in case" requests?

The "How-to Guide to Getting Prayers Answered" is
simple: we just have to sincerely believe He will listen to
us. How can we truly have that level of faith today?

Laid Back

May those You bless be *blessed* and those you curse be cursed.

Numbers 24:9

Blessings and curses aren't just ideas from fairytales; we just don't recognize or count the many blessings we receive from God daily. If we weren't *blessed* every day, our lives would be intolerable. In fact, each day is a *blessing*,[80] because our life is in God's hands.

When we get frustrated, it's important to remember God is ultimately in control. He never makes a mistake, and He loved us enough to sacrifice His only Son for us. Those He blesses are *blessed,* even though we may not feel *blessed* right now.

Still, faith means waiting on Him because God is not a fast-food restaurant. His *blessings* are like fine dining, served at the perfect time. Lay back, be patient, and appreciate His *blessings* when they come.

Who knows what He has in mind for dessert today!

Go Figure!

Blessed are the meek, for they will inherit the earth.

Matthew 5:5

The meek inherit the Earth, not the strong or the aggressive. Go figure! This seems to be the opposite of how things work in the "real" world, but it is exactly how God's kingdom works.

The definition of "meek" is modest, not boastful, and patient under suffering. These are qualities we need for God to work through us.

Meek people admit they need God, and proud people don't. The glory belongs to God, and He uses the meek to demonstrate that *He* won the victory, no one else. God is always in charge, and the sooner we acknowledge that the more we'll accomplish. We are only going to triumph if we are willing to give God control, and that requires meekness.

Humility refers to an attitude you take on yourself; meekness refers to an attitude you show towards others. Meek also means mild.

Try being that mild today.

Last Laugh

Blessed are you who weep now, for you will laugh.

Luke 6:21

Laughter is good medicine. Relaxing our busy and stressed minds while we enjoy something funny that makes us laugh is good for our soul. Sometimes we can laugh with a friend until our ribs ache.

Laughter is a very human trait, but since we are created in God's image, He must laugh, too. Jesus told us to be joyful and used humorous exaggerations like telling us to remove the plank from our eye so we can see to take the speck from our brother's eye.[81]

Even if our life has us weeping now, Jesus assures us in this verse we will laugh when we are with Him in Heaven.

Laughing at life is easier said than done.

Let's try to find a way to laugh at ourselves today.

Easier Said Than Done

Bless those who persecute you...

Romans 12:14

There are many Bible verses about forgiveness. Christ commands it, and He told Peter to forgive seventy times. We know this is easier said than done. We're human and get hurt emotionally, physically, and financially, yet we often forgive strangers sooner than we forgive family and friends. This is because family and friends are supposed to love us, or at least like us, enough to avoid hurting us.

When Paul wrote this verse, He had been stoned, whipped, and beaten by the same people he was urging his followers to *bless*. He was the first to admit he couldn't do it on his own; only the Holy Spirit living within Paul gave him the grace and courage to do so.

Paul is telling us to bless those who hurt and frustrate us, too. On our own, we can't, but with Jesus, we can. Jesus was the example Paul, and the other disciples followed, and the Holy Spirit gave them the strength they needed to bless their enemies.

Blessing those who hurt us takes courage and meekness: the more we practice, the better we will get at it.

Try it out today, and with Jesus's help, it will be easier done than said.

Paid in Full

Blessed is the one whose sin the Lord will never count against them.

Romans 4:8

We get away with plenty, don't we? Maybe it's a warning instead of a speeding ticket or an "edgy" item on our tax return that wasn't challenged. When we add envy, lust, jealousy, gossip, selfishness, and greed to our sin lists, we should appreciate God's mercy much more.

God knows we have sinned, and we are going to sin again and again (and again). Jesus took our penalty with Him to the cross. He hung it on the cross and left it there. This is just like when a speeding fine has been paid—the issue is finished.

While severe consequences often flow from sin, there is no eternal fine or prison for those who believe in Jesus's divinity and confess their sins.

All our sins have been paid for. Thankfully, Jesus is the receipt for sin today, yesterday, tomorrow, and forever.

King's Ransom

Blessed be the king of Israel.

John 12:13

Kings, queens, politicians, and billionaires have constant police and security protection. There may be people or groups who want to kidnap them for ransom. What sort of ransom would be paid for the return of the Queen of England? Better yet, what sort of ransom would be paid for us if we were kidnapped?

The question really is: "What are we worth?"

We weren't kidnapped, but we were lost to God through sin, and there was nothing we could do to get back to Him. God had to pay a ransom to get us back—we couldn't. The price to get us back was the life of God's only Son.

Jesus paid the price for our release.

God paid *the* King's ransom for us. Can we show our thanks for that and all of our other blessings today?

Share the Blame

Blessed are you when people insult you, persecute you and falsely say all kinds of evil against you because of Me.

Matthew 5:11

Nobody likes being blamed for anything, even when we occasionally mess up and deserve it. It is twice as bad when we are blamed for something we didn't do; it feels like a great injustice, and we will strongly defend ourselves from false accusations.

In this sermon, Jesus is preparing us for when we are blamed for any number of things just because we follow Him. He clearly says we will be falsely charged with committing all sorts of evil.

In the first century, Christians were accused of cannibalism for "eating Christ's body" in communion. They were called atheists for not worshipping the Roman gods, and rumors were spread they were incestuous because they "loved" their brothers and sisters.

By following Jesus, trouble will come, ready or not. Are we ready for it today?

Poor Relation

Blessed are the poor in spirit, for theirs is the kingdom of heaven.

Matthew 5:3

While most people have to work hard for what they get, the rich and famous seem to live lives of leisure. In the eyes of our culture, they are the ones who are *blessed*.

Jesus says the poor in spirit inherit His kingdom because those who are poor in spirit are people who recognize they are in need of God's help. As for those who think they have it all, the saying goes, "You can't give directions to someone who doesn't think they're lost."

Wealth often leads to pride, and proud people believe they've caused their own success. The poor in spirit know we're not in control of our lives and need God daily. John said, "those who receive Jesus and believe in His name are God's children."[82]

How can we start becoming poor in spirit today?

Ready to Go

Blessed is the one who does not condemn himself by what he approves.

Romans 14:22

We all like fitting in, but it can often come with a price. Those who ignored the Nazis' treatment of the Jews were just as responsible. We would all like to think we wouldn't stand idly by in the face of evil, but we succumb to group pressure frequently. There are many evils going on in the world, but most of us just shake our heads and do nothing.

It has been said that all it takes for evil to flourish is for good men to do nothing.

We're responsible for our behavior and sins. Paul warns us to avoid places where sin lurks because we are often too weak to reject the temptation. Regular study of Scripture, a change in habits, and earnest prayer are ways to avoid sin and self-condemnation, but we have to want to change first.

How can we stop doing what condemns us and start doing what builds us up today?

Role Model

He replied, *"Blessed* rather are those who hear
the word of God and obey it."

Luke 11:28

Ralph Waldo Emerson said, "Your actions speak so loudly, I can't hear what you are saying." Kids catch on to this quickly and are more likely to behave the way we prefer when we follow our own rules. We can never stop being good role models because any crack in a parent's armor could influence even their adult children's behavior.

Jesus doesn't have any illusions of how godly we are because He knows our heart. Most people don't see our faults because we are good at concealing them. Hearing Jesus's words and ignoring them is the same as outright rejection and rebellion.

We hear, but we don't want to obey.

Hearing and obeying God's word is simple, smart, and sacred.

If we hear His word and obey, we will be blessed. How can we do a better job of that today?

Say It Ain't So

When Esau heard his father's words, he burst out with a loud and bitter cry and said to his father, "*bless* me—me too father!"

Genesis 27:34

Pain is a part of life. We run from it, medicate it, and will do just about anything to avoid it. Physical pain can be excruciating, but it usually stops at some point.

Emotional pain can be overwhelming—and can last a lifetime.

Esau's anguish came from being robbed of his right to his father's *blessing*, but it was really his fault. He lost his blessing because he foolishly gave away his birthright as the eldest son to his younger brother, Jacob.

In the same way, we squander our right to eternal life by not accepting Christ for who He is, our Savior. If we reject Jesus, His Father will reject us, too.

No one comforted Esau, nor will anyone comfort us after such a grave sin. If we choose not to believe that Jesus is our Savior, our pain will be self-inflicted and well-deserved.

There is no better time to choose to follow Jesus than today.

Blind Faith

Then Jesus told him, "Because you have seen me, you have believed; *blessed* are those who have not seen and yet have believed."

John 20:29

The term "seeing is believing" once made sense. Now technology can manufacture sights, sounds, and even smells. Conspiracy theorists question the landing on the moon and the Holocaust, saying the pictures and descriptions of those events are phonies.

Despite all that, we're asked to believe in Jesus, Who lived two thousand years ago and left nothing behind but stories written by His divinely-inspired followers. It takes faith to believe without evidence, but once we take that first step, we find evidence of Jesus all around us.

It is faith that empowers us to say, think, and do things that may put us at risk of rejection, scorn, or worse.

Having faith in Jesus today is certainly not a blind faith, it's eye-opening!

NOVEMBER 2

Forgive and Forget

Blessed are those whose transgressions are forgiven, whose sins are covered.

Romans 4:7

We say we love everyone, but really, we don't. We desire peace, but usually not at the expense of our pride. Forgiving is something we're commanded to do, but we enjoy seeing our enemies squirm and fail. It is human nature, and God wants us to overcome it.

Jesus is our example of how to do that.

He forgave us while we were still sinners, and now it's our turn to forgive those who offend us.

It starts with a prayerful request for help because we will never be able to do it on our own. We're too selfish and self-righteous. We see others' faults as proof of our spiritual superiority, but Jesus spent His time connecting with the misfits and the outcasts of society. He avoided the holier-than-thou people...like us.

Those "losers" genuinely knew they needed His forgiveness. Do we?

Don't say "forgive and forget" today without meaning it.

Nitty Gritty

When one of those at the table with Him heard this, he said to Jesus, *"Blessed* is the one who will eat at the feast in the kingdom of God."

Luke 14:15

Hearing someone spout spiritual-sounding phrases can be irritating. The speaker in this verse is trying to elevate himself above the nitty-gritty of life. Although his words seemed godly, he was really trying to minimize Jesus. Jesus hated arrogance then, and He still hates it now.

Following this verse, Jesus turns the tables on the "holy" men present. He describes a banquet that the "important" people decline to attend; in response, the master fills his dining hall with the poor, blind, and lame.

Jesus tells us to beware of arrogance since only a few will be admitted to His feast.

Jesus came as a Servant and left Earth serving. Are we following His example, or do we demand to be served?

Who can we serve today?

Out of Nowhere

This man, however, did not trace his descent from Levi, yet he collected a tenth from Abraham and *blessed* him who had the promises.

Hebrews 7:6

This man, named Melchizedek, came out of nowhere. Abraham had won a military victory and rescued his nephew Lot. Suddenly, a king named Melchizedek appeared, and Abraham, sensing the man's spiritual superiority, "tithed" to him. Nothing else is known about Melchizedek.

Jesus came out of nowhere, too. He didn't come from a prominent or wealthy family, and His hometown had a bad reputation. What Jesus had was His divinity, which drew people to Him. Fortunately, we don't need a fancy pedigree to enter His presence; in fact, it could hinder us because we wouldn't "need" Him as much. The Holy Spirit wants to be part of our lives, too.

He will come out of nowhere to rescue us today if we just humble ourselves and ask Him to come.

Eat Up

Then the land yields its harvest; God, our God, *blesses* us.

Psalm 67:6

We eat to live, but sometimes, we can also seem to live to eat. It can be as much of an emotional experience as physical. For instance, mothers love to watch their children eat, and men often equate a home-cooked meal with nurturing and love.

This verse isn't really focusing on growing grain; in all actuality, it is about the abundance God wants to shower on those who praise Him. He wants our praise because that is how we show our true love and gratefulness to Him, which is good and necessary for us, as His children.

Love and gratitude differentiate our relationship with Him from all but the absolute closest people in our lives. He wants us to hunger for a depth of connection that reaches into our soul. God wants us to desire a relationship with Him the way a starving man craves food.

Do we just pick at the relationship God offers us, or do we dig in wholeheartedly?

How can we crave Him today?

Trial by Fire

Blessed is the one who perseveres under trial because, having stood the test, that person will receive a crown of life that the Lord has promised to those who love Him.

James 1:12

Perseverance is in short supply today. We change aspects of our lives as fast as we flip through TV channels. It is much easier to switch jobs, houses, and spouses than ever before. We change our opinions, beliefs, and political parties in the blink of an eye, all the time.

James's life was radically different from ours. He and many other Christians were being severely persecuted, and when confronted with death or torture, a victim of the Roman army had an easy-out: they could deny Christ, sacrifice to Roman idols, and live unmolested.

That's a powerful argument, and many chose that option. Others refused to deny Jesus and were tortured and died for their faith. *Our* faith.

How will we respond to the trials by fire we may experience today?

Right on Time

Then I heard a voice from heaven say, "Write this: *blessed* are the dead who die in the Lord from now on." "Yes," says the Spirit, "they will rest from their labor, for their deeds will follow them."

Revelation 14:13

If we knew the date of our death, we would most likely live our life very differently. Whether we would live better lives, though, would all depend on what we understand "better" to mean.

For many people, better might be more travel or leisure. Others might opt for time with their family. Without a greater sense of purpose, some would spend their remaining days in drunkenness and debauchery. A few would try as much as possible, however, to bring others to a knowledge of Christ. This is because they'd know their time was short.

The second half of this verse tells us our deeds will follow us. Would we make different decisions with those words in mind? Like it or not, God doesn't need to share certain information with us. Whether death comes slowly or suddenly, one thing is for sure: God is always right on time.

He will come for some of us today, right on time. Are we ready?

Power-Up

Now that you know these things, you will be
blessed if you do them.

John 13:17

Living in the information age means we don't have
to go to a library, flip through the card catalog, pull the
right book from the shelf, and read until we find our answer. We have Google on our phone. In less time than
it took to read the last sentence, we'd be well on the way
to having the answer to almost any question we could
think of. Gaining knowledge is quick and easy today.

What did Jesus want His apostles to know? He had
just washed their feet to demonstrate they were to be
servants, not masters, and that God vastly values humility more than pride or self-satisfaction. We look to
His example for the answer.

Jesus came to serve, and that's what He wants us to
do.

Knowledge is power.

How are we going to put our knowledge of Jesus into
action today?

Be Careful Out There

Scripture foresaw that God would justify the Gentiles by faith, and announced the gospel in advance to Abraham: "All nations will be *blessed* through you."

Galatians 3:8

In the film *It's a Wonderful Life*, George experienced what his hometown would have been like without him. It was eye-opening, and he saw how much his life had affected others.

What would our world be like if Jesus hadn't come to Earth? Would we still be worshipping Roman idols? Would it be as caring of a place without His command to love others? Would the less fortunate be integrated into society without His message of equality and humility?

We know, though, that Jesus's life on this Earth was real, His place in history is undeniable, and the evidence for this is very observable. God has given us free will to choose. The question is: are we going to believe it, deny it, or take the easiest way out and ignore it?

God told Moses to tell the Israelites they must make a choice between life and death, then He urged them to choose life.[83]

Pray the Holy Spirit will help us to make all the right choices today.

Back to the Future

By faith Isaac *blessed* Jacob and Esau in regard to their future.

Hebrews 11:20

The future is always hazy and uncertain. We think back on the changes that have occurred during our lifetime with hope and fear for the future. Hope because there are now cures for the previously incurable illnesses, peace between former enemy countries, and inventions that have made life a lot easier. Despite those advances, we can be frightened because many cultural changes threaten our sense of right and wrong.

Christianity is under attack.

We don't like uncertainty, regardless of how rosy some predictions may be. Regardless, Jesus, Who is with us now, is from our past and in our future. God said He has plans to prosper us and not to harm us,[84] so having faith in the future means having faith in Christ.

Don't worry about the future.

Only worry about how to love Him and others today.

Lifted Up

When He had led them out to the vicinity of Bethany, He lifted up His hands and *blessed* them.

Luke 24:50

This verse describes the last time Jesus was physically present on Earth. He had been with His disciples for forty days since His resurrection, and He told them He would send the Holy Spirit to guide them.

The apostles believed Jesus and had faith. They trusted and obeyed His every word. They went back to Jerusalem, elected a replacement for Judas, then waited and prayed. Ten days later, the Holy Spirit came rushing down from Heaven like the sound of a violent wind and filled the upper room during the festival of Pentecost.

God was faithful to His word.

He may sometimes change our direction to develop our relationship with Him, and while we may not know why things happen, we can always trust it is for our good.

Little children like to be lifted up so they can see things better.

Pray the Spirit will lift us up to see Him better today.

Human Nature

Praise be to the God and Father of our Lord Jesus Christ, who has *blessed* us in the heavenly realms with every spiritual *blessing* in Christ.

Ephesians 1:3

What exactly are spiritual *blessings*? We know what material *blessings* look like, and usually, those are what we ask for when we pray; after all, it is human nature to ask for God's provision.

Spiritual *blessings* are a little trickier. They are things that don't come naturally for us, like faith, hope, love, and humility. Naturally, we are either gullible or skeptical, selfless or greedy, proud or timid. Jesus modeled how we should live in both the material and spiritual worlds.

Discipline and prayer are the two ways to pursue spiritual *blessings*.

We know there are temptations that will try to drag us back, but through diligent discipline and earnest prayer, Christ will rescue us.

Spiritual *blessings* are real, and they are accessible. Pray to receive them today.

Promised Land

Land that drinks in the rain often falling on it and that produces a crop useful to those for whom it is farmed receives the *blessing* of God.

Hebrews 6:7

God's love is unlimited! We notice only a tiny fraction of the *blessings* He showers on us. Some of the *blessings* we receive in our country are medical advances like bypass surgery and cures for various types of cancer or infections. Other diseases like smallpox, and soon, polio, have been completely eradicated. To that extent, our modern world is like the Promised Land.

Also, famine is, at best, an afterthought; we never miss a meal. Our land has been *blessed* by the only One who can give us the abundance we have. While there are many evil forces at play, too, God's promises to us are yes and amen.[85] This means they're a sure thing.

Take five minutes and list just a few of them today.

Peace on Earth

is the King who comes in the Name of the Lord!

Luke 19:38

World peace usually makes people think of nations living together in harmony. Unfortunately, world peace is somewhat built upon "mutually assured destruction:" we can wipe each other out with nuclear weapons, so nobody wants to start any real trouble.

During the holidays, peace in families is a goal as people living different lives have to behave and act civilly towards each other. In this setting, peace means patience.

Christ didn't come to bring either of those kinds of peace, and He explicitly said so. We find God's peace by seeking to know Him and then following His directions. As we spend time with God, we feel His peace saturate our being; it seeps deep into our soul, giving us the assurance of our salvation.[86]

Today, pray for the peace of God which passes all understanding.[87]

Slip and Fall

Blessed is anyone who does not stumble on account of me.

Luke 7:23

Being balanced can refer to physical balance, the kind athletes have, and older people lose. Another use of the word is when we eat a balanced diet in an effort to be healthier. Having a balanced view of life usually becomes easier as we age; often, the stridency of youth mellows as life becomes less black and white.

In this verse, Jesus gave John the Baptist's followers a loving rebuke, saying that even if Jesus's ministry did not exactly match their expectations, John and his followers must be open to God's unfolding plan.

We need to fit into God's plan for our lives, not try to fit God into ours. If we try to decide what the best route for our life is, many things will try to knock us off our spiritual balance beam. Temptations of all kinds can trip us up and turn our focus from God to things like success, materialism, and unhealthy relationships.

Being His follower isn't easy or smooth, and the road's narrow.

Let's watch all of our steps today.

Hit the Road

Blessed is she who has believed that the Lord would fulfill his promises to her.

Luke 1:45

Travel these days is fairly easy. Manned spacecraft fly around the world on a daily basis, and a road trip that would have taken our forefathers a week to complete now takes us an hour.

In this verse, Mary was visiting her cousin, Elizabeth. Mary was a poor, unmarried, and pregnant girl, and God gave her a vision about her baby (and of the baby that her much older cousin, Elizabeth, was carrying). Mary believed God's promise and traveled the long, hard journey from Nazareth to Elizabeth's home to share in the good news they both had received.

What faith and commitment this shows—and to think, sometimes we're tempted to skip church on Sunday, even though it is a relatively short drive! James said, "Faith without deeds is useless,"[88] and Mary demonstrates this wisdom.

How can we take our faith with us when we hit the road today?

What's It Worth

By faith Jacob, when he was dying, *blessed* each of Joseph's sons, and worshiped as he leaned on the top of his staff.

Hebrews 11:21

Inheritances are often spent fairly quickly on things that don't last and won't be remembered. The idea of leaving a "legacy" usually means hoping some tiny memory of us will endure for more than a generation; statistically speaking, a generation is only twenty-five years.

Jacob wanted to reward his son Joseph for rescuing the family from famine. Unfortunately, Joseph's descendants turned out to be a huge force of wickedness in Israel. What we learn from this is that only God is good, and He knows the future. God's word tells us everyone has sinned and fallen short of His standard.[89]

We chase after wealth, health, and everything temporary, things that don't hold their worth. The only permanent things we can hold onto are our faith, hope, and love in Jesus.

If we are honest with ourselves, we know that a very high price was paid for eternal life, Jesus' death on the cross. The real question for us is what we going to do today, by our words, attitudes and deeds, to show others that we are worth that price.

Heir Apparent

And you are heirs of the prophets and of the covenant God made with your fathers. He said to Abraham, "Through your offspring all peoples on earth will be *blessed*."

Acts 3:25

Inheritances are great. To those who receive them, they're free money; someone else had to work for and worry about it. We receive it because we're related to the deceased, but this also means someone died.

Jesus died so we could have a Heavenly inheritance.

Adoption is the process of taking someone who doesn't share the family DNA and giving them all the rights of natural children, including inheritance rights.

We're not physically related to Abraham, but we're his adopted heirs. We're adopted when we believe that his Father is also our Father, displaying faith in God. That makes us heirs of God's kingdom.

Don't squander this inheritance.

How can we invest it in the lives of those around us today?

Wimp Out

"If you, Israel, will return, then return to me,"
declares the Lord. "If you put your detestable
idols out of my sight and no longer go astray,
and if in a truthful, just and righteous way
you swear, 'As surely as the Lord lives,' then
the nations will invoke blessing by Him and
in Him they will boast.'"

Jeremiah 4:1-2

Our idols aren't made of wood and stone. They are
things we choose over God, things we love, and unin-
tentionally worship.

God knows we are weak, but He continues to forgive us. Jesus knows when we're spiritual wimps. We
try, and we fail, then we try again, and we fail again. He
knows we're going to wimp out.

The apostle Peter denied Jesus three times, but eventually stood his ground for Him and later led the early
church. Confessing our sin is key to receiving forgiveness and growing in strength.

How can we stop wimping out and take a stand for
Jesus today?

Press On

As you know, we count as *blessed* those who have persevered.

James 5:11

We hear about perseverance from coaches and athletes all the time. They talk about the preparation and diligent effort needed to win. As inspiring as it may be, this inspiration is temporary, it takes a Google search to remember who won the Super Bowl ten years ago.

In this verse, James has his attention on a more profound type of perseverance: maintaining our faith in the face of serious persecution. Most of us have not faced that sort of discrimination yet, but he is warning us to be prepared. Whenever it happens, we won't be alone. Millions of Christians have suffered, and are suffering, for their faith.

Will we feel like we're being *blessed* when we are being threatened, like them? We're not training to receive a medal or trophy; we're training to receive eternal life and be a role model for those around us.

The only motivation to keep pressing on in suffering is a deep and personal relationship with God.

Begin working on that today.

First Among Equals

Each of you must bring a gift in proportion
to the way the Lord your God has *blessed* you.
Deuteronomy 16:17

We like to imagine we all start out as equal, but there is nothing equal about one child being born in a ghetto and another being born to parents who belong to a country club. Their opportunities are not likely to ever be equal. Children born in third-world countries won't have the education or opportunities that babies born in first-world countries will enjoy.

With Jesus, everyone who believes in Him is equal. Equality begins when we surrender our lives to Him; then, no matter where we come from or what we look like, He loves us equally and is happy to admit us into His kingdom.

He wants us to surrender the control of our lives to Him.

Are we equal to that task today?

The Truth Hurts

Then Simeon *blessed* them and said to Mary
His mother: "This child is destined to cause
the falling and the rising of many in Israel,
and to be a sign that will be spoken against,
so that the thoughts of many hearts will be revealed. And a sword will pierce your soul too."
Luke 2:34-35

What a bittersweet verse! As good Jewish parents,
Mary and Joseph are presenting their firstborn son to
the Lord. Simeon, a prophet, tells them their Son's des-
tiny is one of both hope and suffering and then adds
that He will be the cause of suffering for Mary, too.

These days, most people are skeptical about what to
believe is true; "fake news" and false advertising is everywhere. The truth is, though, Jesus is God, and there
is no other way to Heaven except through Him. Many
don't accept this, and some actively oppose it.

When would we want to discover that truth? Today?

Tried and True

So those who rely on faith are *blessed* along with Abraham, the man of faith.

Galatians 3:9

Something is tried and true when it's been tested by time and hardship. Many people own the same car for years because they find it reliable. That doesn't mean it hasn't had mechanical problems; once it's running again, though, they trust it to get them where they're going.

Abraham is the tried and true guy of the Old Testament. Based on God's promise, he waited until he was a hundred years old to become Isaac's father. Abraham's level of faith is breathtaking, and Paul is saying the faith Abraham had is available to us too. Jesus said we can move mountains and uproot trees if we have the tiniest bit of faith.

How many of us have tested that? Our faith is strengthened when we apply it.

Are we prepared to maintain faith for a hundred years?

How about trying to get all the way through today?

Tit-for-Tat

For I know that whoever you *bless* is *blessed*,
and whoever you curse is cursed.

Numbers 22:6

The Israelites left Egypt, had been in the desert for forty years and were set to enter the Promised Land. A king from the neighboring country of Moab was afraid of them and hired Balaam to curse them. God didn't let him curse Israel; He told him to bless them instead.

God watches out for us too, and not just for the big issues we struggle with. He cares about the small ones, as well. Jesus took the curses that should have been ours to the cross. Unlike Balaam, whoever God wants to *bless* is *blessed*, and He *blesses* us much more than we deserve.

Trust God with the small things today, and He will take care of the big ones too.

Full-Strength

Blessed is the one whom God corrects; so do
not despise the discipline of the Almighty.

Job 5:17

No one likes being punished. We're alright with seeing others get their due, but somehow, our faults are *understandable*. We claim God's full-strength justice for the guilty, but His mercy toward ourselves. We see our sins as trivial and theirs as deserving of God's wrath.

When God corrects us for our sins, He does it for our own good (as any parent does). He certainly receives no satisfaction from it. Without correction, we wouldn't change and would run headlong into disaster. The bottom line is we are weak, and God has to shake us up. He must remind us when we're wrong and move us into His will again. This teaches us to shift away from the acceptance of our own sins.

He always wants our full-strength compliance.

God wants obedience, not excuses, today.

Try It! You'll Like It

For the grace of God has appeared that offers salvation to all people. It teaches us to say "no" to ungodliness and worldly passions, and to live self-controlled, upright and godly lives in this present age, while we wait for the *blessed* hope—the appearing of the glory of our great God and Savior, Jesus Christ, who gave Himself for us to redeem us from all wickedness and to purify for Himself a people that are His very own, eager to do what is good.

Titus 2:11-14

We usually don't value things we receive for free; we think there must be a catch or some sort of trick. Often, there is—not in this verse, though.

God offers salvation for free to everyone who believes His Son Jesus died for our sins. It's as simple as that. We move from a life of self-centeredness and worldly passions to a life that is self-controlled, upright, and Godly.

God purifies us for Himself so that we are eager to do what is good.

His offer of salvation to us today is free and easy. If you haven't done so before, try it. You'll like it!

Playing with Fire

Afterward, as you know, when he wanted to inherit this *blessing*, he was rejected.

Hebrews 12:17

Jesus died for our sins, and when we choose to make Him Lord over every area in our life, all our sins are forgiven. Yet, how many people really do that? How many willingly surrender their whole life to His dominion?

Very few.

We like to think we're in control, and we ask ourselves: "What's the worst that could happen?"

The answer is worse than you may think.

In this verse, Esau forfeited his father's *blessing*, like many people forfeit God's *blessings*. Things like greed, envy, or lust do not cause us to forfeit salvation—ignoring God, as Esau did, does.

Later in Hebrews, God is called a consuming fire, and consuming fires are awesome, awful, and unstoppable.

Get right with God today. Don't get burned!

Winners Never Quit

Blessed are those who are persecuted because of righteousness, for theirs is the kingdom of heaven.

Matthew 5:10

We all generally want to be well-liked by those around us, and the peer pressure we feel often makes us want to go along with the crowd. That's fine if it's the right crowd, and they behave in a manner that is in line with our views. On the other hand, what if the people we associate with move in a direction that we're uncomfortable with or that we think is wrong?

That's where persecution can start.

We may not be physically or even psychologically threatened, but we certainly may be excluded from group activities. We may even be turned down for a job or promotion if our Christian lifestyle doesn't fit in with the company "culture." Jesus is telling us not to be surprised and to even feel blessed because of it.

Jesus didn't win any popularity contests, and neither will we if we uphold righteousness.

We will, however, win salvation.

Winners never quit. Don't quit standing up for your faith today.

Tough Guy

Then Joshua *blessed* Caleb son of Jephunneh
and gave him Hebron as his inheritance.

Joshua 14:13

Caleb is the John Wayne-type tough guy of the Bible.
When Moses sent twelve men to explore the Promised
Land, Caleb went, and he was already forty years old!
Of the twelve, only he and Joshua wanted to go into the
land and take it by force. At eighty years old, he helped
conquer Canaan as a warrior, and at eighty-five, he was
still fighting God's enemies.

Caleb was *blessed* because he loved and feared God.

We may love and fear God, but even traffic can
stress us out. Caleb is a role model in every sense, but
especially as a person who was willing to sacrifice everything for God. Caleb's life wasn't motivated by personal comfort; he lived focused on God's will for his life.

Being a warrior for God may not always be easy or
comfortable, but we will always be victorious.

Toughen up today.

Get Real

For the time will come when you will say, "*Blessed* are the childless women, the wombs that never bore and the breasts that never nursed!"

Luke 23:29

Christians tend to dress up bad news. We talk about joy and love, and we want to share the *blessings* that flow from being a part of God's family. What we almost never talk about, though, is hell and the end of the world.

We "hide the ball" about these topics, either because we don't want to come across as a "fire and brimstone" person or because we really aren't convinced that our close, non-Christian friends and family members are doomed if they are not persuaded of Christ's saving message.

Jesus always gets real. He never hides the ball, and He says what needs to be said.

In this verse, Jesus is describing the suffering that will come in the end times. He knew hiding this from people won't change or delay it. Hearing about the end may just help others make the eternally critical decision to follow Jesus.

It may sound awful, but it's true, and it could happen soon.

Let's get real with others today!

Wrap-Up

I know that when I come to you, I will come in
the full measure of the *blessing* of Christ.

Romans 15:29

How are we planning to wrap up our lives? Do we
want physical perfection? Minimal wrinkles? A firm,
tight, and fit body? Are we striving for financial fitness?
Having all the money our family will need so that a good
life is "guaranteed?"

How about emotional fitness? That's when we worry
about ourselves and our family while forgetting that
God holds everything in *His* hands.

In this verse, Paul is planning to visit Rome. He
didn't know that when he finally arrived, he would be a
chained prisoner—and we don't know what the future
holds for us, either. His message changed dramatically
between his letter to the Romans and his second letter
to Timothy when he realized that his death was not far
off.

How do we want the wrap-up of our lives to be?
Comfortable or committed? Rest or risk? We have to
decide today.

Make Nice

When we are cursed, we *bless*; when we are persecuted, we endure it; when we are slandered, we answer kindly. We have become the scum of the earth, the garbage of the world—right up to this moment.

1 Corinthians 4: 12-13

Psychology has given us the "flight or fight" theory. It says that when we are threatened, we either run away or fight back. Instead of road rage, it's usually easier to move to another lane and let the idiot go around us. When we're physically threatened, we can either call 911 or prepare to do battle.

Paul's beliefs were threatened, yet he didn't fight or flee.

He *blessed*.

Can we do that? Not on our own, but with Christ, all things are possible.[90] To endure what Paul did and still bless our persecutors, we need the strength of Jesus, and that is when Jesus makes us strongest.

In *West Side Story*, Riff says he is only going to a dance with his gang's rivals, the Sharks, to "make nice." Let's do our best to make nice today.

No Muss, No Fuss

In the sight of God, who gives life to everything, and of Christ Jesus, who while testifying before Pontius Pilate made the good confession, I charge you to keep this command without spot or blame until the appearing of our Lord Jesus Christ, which God will bring about in His own time—God, the *blessed* and only Ruler, the King of kings and Lord of lords, who alone is immortal and who lives in unapproachable light, whom no one has seen or can see. To Him be honor and might forever. Amen.

1 Timothy 6:13-16

In this passage, Paul is telling Timothy not to be afraid of proclaiming the truth. This is sometimes scary and often inconvenient. Jesus is God, and there is no other path to the Father except through Jesus. When Jesus said He is the Way, the Truth, and the Life,[91] He meant it. No muss, no fuss. Simple, but serious.

We need to follow Paul's advice given to Timothy and stand firm in our convictions.

It is hard to keep our walk with God without spot or blemish or without blame or shame. Can we do that today?

Go For It

But whoever looks intently into the perfect
law that gives freedom, and continues in it—
not forgetting what they have heard, but doing it—they will be *blessed* in what they do.

James 1:25

Sometimes we meet people who tell us their name,
but we immediately forget it because we aren't paying
attention. Often, these people aren't all that important
to us, and we're really just being polite.

In this verse, James warns us that it's easy to receive
God's word, immediately forget it, and go on with our
lives just like before. James later says it's like looking in
a mirror and then forgetting what we look like. He is
urging us to remember what we hear by doing what we
heard. If we are Jesus's followers, we need to walk with
Him, not just read about Him.

The time to get off the couch and go into His world
is today. Go for it!

Turn Around

When God raised up His Servant, He sent
Him first to you to *bless* you by turning each
of you from your wicked ways.

Acts 3:26

People don't think of themselves as wicked. We
imagine that there are evil people, but generally, we
hope they are either in prison or far away.

In this verse, Peter is telling his countrymen they
are wicked and need to turn their lives around. Some of
those listening may have been swept up with the crowd
that crucified Jesus, while others probably stayed quiet
and watched.

Their real sin was not accepting Jesus as the Messiah, and many of us may not truly believe that, either.
John says that when we deny that Jesus is God, we are
calling God a liar.[92]

A Turkish proverb says, "No matter how far down
the wrong road you have gone, turn back."

We need to decide what we believe and then turn
our lives around.

Straddling the middle of the road is very dangerous.

Making a U-turn may be the smartest move we can
make today.

Mission Control

And Mary said: "My soul glorifies the Lord and my spirit rejoices in God my Savior, for He has been mindful of the humble state of His servant. From now on all generations will call me *blessed*, for the Mighty One has done great things for me—holy is His Name."

Luke 1:46-49

Mary was a poor, young virgin. There was nothing that made her the obvious choice for the job of becoming Jesus's mother, trusted with the mission to raise Him into a man.

That's how God does it, though: He doesn't want us to think we're in control of anything. He just wants our unquestioned obedience. That is what He got from Mary when she was told how her life would be changed.

He's given each of us a mission and a purpose, but discovering what that is isn't easy. However, it always starts with giving complete control of our lives to Him, as Mary did.

Who is in control of today's mission?

Key to Success

So he said, "I am Abraham's servant. The Lord
has *blessed* my master abundantly, and he has
become wealthy."

Genesis 24:34-35

In the Old Testament, wealth is often seen as God's
blessing. It may have been due to leading a more righteous life, like Abraham, or it could have been the result of being in the right place at the right time, like
Solomon. The New Testament doesn't condemn riches,
but it urges the good management of our God-given
finances.

Having plenty of money and possessions doesn't
disqualify us from entering Heaven; it's the false sense
of security it brings, though, that can lead us to dependency on ourselves and away from God.

Jesus said it's easier for a camel to go through the
eye of a needle than for a rich man to enter the Kingdom of Heaven.[93] This is because usually, only those in
need seek Him. Jesus came to save the lost, not those
who are only searching for success.

The key to success is trusting God in all things today.

Mountain Climbing

It is as if the dew of Hermon were falling on Mount Zion. For there the Lord bestows His *blessings*, even life forevermore.

Psalm 133:3

Mount Hermon is the highest mountain in both Syria and Israel. It's almost ten thousand feet high, and its lofty peak attracts plenty of moisture. Mount Zion is a desert mountain, barely twenty-five-hundred feet high. If Hermon's dew fell on Mount Zion, it would be a great blessing.

This psalm is really about brotherly love. God *blesses* brothers and sisters who live together in harmony, but there can only be unity and harmony according to God's terms. All religions are not equal, and attempts to make us all "brothers" will always fail.

Jesus said He is the only Way; He didn't hedge or hesitate when He said it. If we want His blessings, we have to acknowledge our sin and dependence on Him.

We'll reach the top of His mountain when we realize we can't climb it alone.

Ask for God's help with each step we take today.

At Risk

The Ark of the Covenant remained with the family of Obed-Edom in his house for three months, and the Lord *blessed* his household and everything he had.

1 Chronicles 13:14

Most of us love action. Whether we are active "thrill-seekers" or we just like to watch stunts on TV, the lure of peril and danger is addictive. Modern missionaries embody the essence of bold living. They take their families to remote places and expose them to a significant measure of risk to help spread God's word.

We are not all called to go overseas; our ministry may be here. Either way, we are called to risk our pride and comfort to share God's word with others.

Obed-Edom was given custody of the ark because no one else dared to take it; after all, a man had just mishandled it and was struck dead. Obed-Edom was willing to take the risk of accepting the Ark anyway, though, and God *blessed* him for it.

There are precious few times when God asks us to take big risks for Him.

Is today one of those times?

Glory Days

Blessed be Your glorious name, and may it be exalted above all *blessing* and praise.

Nehemiah 9:5

Bruce Springsteen made the term "Glory Days" famous. His legendary song is about people in high school who were enjoying the "peak" of their lives but never moved beyond that phase of life. Often we see our glory days as being in the past. Whether they were *actually* better days or just the memories of a seemingly better time is debatable.

In this verse, Nehemiah is glorifying God for *blessing* His people despite their sins. We all sin, and some sins are more evident than others, but if we confess our sins and turn away from those ways, God will forgive us.[94]

God opens the doors of grace and forgiveness, so we don't have to be trapped in our past.

Our glory days are ahead, not behind us.

Our glory days start today!

Wait Here

While He was *blessing* them, He left them and was taken up into heaven.

Luke 24:51

A few more than forty days before this verse took place, the disciples watched as Jesus was crucified. He was resurrected after three days and was now ascending into Heaven.

What happened?

Everything happened: all the prophecies concerning Jesus were fulfilled. He had conquered death and pain, and most importantly, He had conquered sin, which gave all people a path back to God the Father. His resurrection also proved He was God the Son.

Then His ascension showed the disciples He was going home to Heaven and His Father.

Jesus promised to send the Holy Spirit to guide them, but that wouldn't happen for ten long days. They needed faith to wait for the Holy Spirit, and when He sent it, He filled the disciples with power. Their waiting was rewarded.

Jesus gave us the same instructions: to tell the world about Him and to obey His teachings. That takes faith and courage, which is why He sent the Holy Spirit to us.

Can we be patient and wait for Him to act in our lives today?

Hidden Jewels

Look, your house is left to you desolate. I tell
you, you will not see Me again until you say,
"Blessed is He who comes in the name of the
Lord."

Luke 13:35

God doesn't pick the same people we would for a
task. While we would always go for the smart, attractive
ones, He takes the excluded people and makes them
into jewels, just like He did with us.

The people of Jerusalem were looking for a smart,
attractive Messiah: a warrior to overthrow the Romans.
What they got was a regular-looking man who didn't
seem to have any desire to fight the Romans. He did
have the power, but He was meek.

And so they rejected Him, their real Messiah, a Dia-
mond in the rough! God doesn't wrap salvation up like
a Christmas present. It's packaged in love, pain, and
faith.

When we open His gift of eternal life, we begin a celebration that lasts an eternity.

Don't be a hidden jewel.

How can we show God's sparkle in everything we do
today?

Haves and Have-nots

And without a doubt, the lesser is *blessed* by
the greater.

Hebrews 7:7

Status plays a subtle role in our lives. Most countries
don't have formal ranks, like those with monarchies
do, or a caste system where birth determines everything about a person's life. But western cultures still
have plenty of haves and have-nots. Although it allows
movement between classes, hard work and good ideas
are usually needed to make a difference.

In this verse, the writer of Hebrews is retelling how
Abraham was blessed by his spiritual superior, the mysterious Melchizedek. But Jesus isn't mysterious, and
He's more than our spiritual superior, He's our God. He
introduced the revolutionary concept that all people are
equal in God's sight. Women, who had been perpetually
oppressed in ancient times, were just as entitled to receive God's *blessings* as men; slaves were of equal spiritual rank as their masters.

Through faith in Jesus, we can all have all His *blessings* now.

Let's take what we have and share it with the have-
nots today.

Take Your Pick

Esau said, "Isn't he rightly called Jacob? This is the second time he has taken advantage of me: He took my birthright, and now he's taken my *blessing!*"

Genesis 27:36

Life is an endless series of choices. Most are minor, but others just *seem* trivial. Many of the biggest decisions we make don't seem important at the time, but later have monumental results.

Esau is experiencing the effect of choices here. He voluntarily gave up his birthright and inheritance for a bowl of stew. Jacob then decided to deliberately steal his brother's *blessing*. The choices of both men had lifelong consequences for them and their family.

We only have one real decision to make: do we accept Christ as our Savior, or are we going to inwardly deny His promise of salvation?

Take your pick today.

Judgment Call

May you be *blessed* for your good judgment and for keeping me from bloodshed this day and from avenging myself with my own hands.

1 Samuel 25:33

God described David as a man "after His own heart."[95] He was full of God's wisdom, intensity, and sensitivity.

In this verse, God is protecting David from himself. David is angry because he had been humiliated. He's on his way to take revenge when God intervenes and keeps him from tragedy.

God is always doing that for us, too, because we're often our own worst enemies. Usually, our impulse to lash out at others stems from nothing more than a bruised ego. God avenged David later, and He protects us in the same way.

He'll fight our battles and rescue us from others, especially from ourselves and the sometimes foolish decisions we make.

We can be men and women after God's own heart like David was, but this means we must also strive to be courageous, faithful, and patient.

Pray we'll make the right judgment calls today.

Follow the Leader

The crowds that went ahead of Him and those that followed shouted, "Hosanna to the Son of David! *Blessed* is He who comes in the name for the Lord! Hosanna in the highest."

Matthew 21:9

Jesus sometimes enters biblical scenes purposefully, though, at other times, He is subtle, like when He went to Jerusalem secretly because His time hadn't yet come. Often, His entries are dramatic: the angels announcing His birth, the Holy Spirit appearing at His baptism, and here when He's coming to Jerusalem days before His crucifixion.

How do we announce Jesus to those around us? Subtlety may work, but it shouldn't be used as a substitute for cowardice. Boldness may be the only way to go, but being obnoxious or weird doesn't win converts, either. As the Beatles said, "If you go around carrying pictures of Chairman Mao, you ain't going to make it with anyone anyhow."

We need to pray for discernment and courage and ask the Holy Spirit to guide us and show us when opportunities to share with people present themselves.

Smart people are willing to be led; show them the perfect Leader.

Be smart. Follow the Leader today.

Wide Receiver

In everything I did, I showed you that by this
kind of hard work we must help the weak, remembering the words the Lord Jesus Himself
said: It is more *blessed* to give than to receive.

Acts 20:35

Jesus isn't into Christmas, He's into people. It's easy
to lose sight of that in the midst of the glitter and celebrating. Jesus's gift is the ultimate gift, eternal life.

Imagine spending your life savings on a present that
is rejected or ignored? It would almost certainly destroy
the relationship, but that's how we often treat Jesus.

Yet, despite the fact that we either reject Him outright or ignore His gifts and blessings, He still loves us
and gives us even more.

The miracle of Christmas isn't only about the baby
in the manger, it is about the mercies He showers on us
all year round.

Look for those today.

Come Clean

Blessed are those who wash their robes, that they may have the right to the tree of life and may go through the gates into the city.

Revelation 22:14

Will next year be the best year of our lives or the worst? Will our health improve, decline, or will we die? Will the country succeed or stumble? Only God knows what it will bring.

This verse appears at the end of the Book of Revelation, where the new, mystical Jerusalem descends from Heaven. Whether it is accurate or symbolic, the question is: who gets in? Jesus repeatedly told us He is the only Way, Truth, and Life—no one comes to the Father except through Him. This means that even Buddha, Mohammad, or Krishna don't get in without accepting Jesus, and neither do their followers.

But He loves us all. We only need to believe in Jesus and come clean about our sins to be saved.

Look back on the year, make a list of God's *blessings*, then give thanks for all of them.

Free for All

They are always generous and lend freely;
their children will be *blessed*.

Psalm 37:26

We're born selfish, and the two-year-old's cry of
"mine" never completely leaves us. We love to say that
we worked hard for what we have, but ultimately, our
success has as much to do with where we were born and
the parents who raised us as anything we've accom-
plished on our own.

God wants us to remember that.

It is His generosity and kindness that has allowed us
to have the health, wealth, and opportunities we enjoy.

The psalmist is describing how righteous people return to God some of what He has *blessed* them with by
being loving, compassionate, and charitable to others.

St. Augustine said, "God has no need for money, but
the poor have. You give it to the poor, and God receives
it."

Give and receive *blessings* generously today.

Promises, Promises

He redeemed us in order that the *blessing* given to Abraham might come to the Gentiles through Christ Jesus, so that by faith we might receive the promise of the Spirit.

Galatians 3:14

Promises are made and broken all the time. Politicians are famous for vowing to do something and then not keeping their word. Employers sometimes promise raises and then do not deliver. A friend will swear to repay a loan but doesn't. When we put our faith in people, we will always be disappointed because when push comes to shove, "I" comes before "U" in the alphabet.

But God always keeps His promises.

He promised that by having faith in Jesus, we would be filled with the Holy Spirit. The Holy Spirit guides believers on how to think, what to say, how to say it, and what to do.

We break promises all too frequently, but God has never broken any of His, and He never will.

To be a Christian means to strive to be Christ-like.

Let's remember that today when a promise is about to be made.

DECEMBER 21

Ethnic Diversity

So they will put My Name on the Israelites,
and I will *bless* them.

Numbers 6:27

Anyone with an unusual name has secretly wished it
was simpler. "Smith" and "Jones" are easy to remember;
everyone can pronounce and spell them. Spelling more
ethnic names presents challenges, especially when
someone is trying to accomplish something over the
phone. It may take the hearer on the other end of the
line several times before they get it right. That's when
we may want to legally change that name!

When we are a part of God's family, we can sometimes have a problem with our names, too. "Christian"
is a term under stress, and the world is growing increasingly hostile towards us. People even use God's
name as a swear word!

In this verse, God is saying that if we take on His
name, we'll be blessed.

Being called Christian may make things difficult,
but wear it like a badge of honor today!

Read It and Weep

Blessed is the one who reads the words of this prophecy.

Revelation 1:3

The Book of Revelation is not one Christians spend their most time reading. It can seem scary, somewhat confusing, and is certainly unsettling, but maybe that's God's point. We need to read it annually to be reminded that *all* of this will come to an end, slowly but surely. The daily concerns we carry around will seem trivial once we know and understand God's master plan, and it's important to remember that He wins!

We also need to remember that Jesus said only the Father knows the day and the hour; not even Jesus knows when it will come. He did, however, say that when His sign appears in the sky, all the nations will mourn because of the coming judgments, and His followers are to "stand up and lift up your heads, because your redemption is drawing near."[96]

Today, don't focus on the end. Let's focus on what we can do to help others we know experience redemption, not condemnation.

King of the Hill

I will *bless* them and the places surrounding
My holy hill.

Ezekiel 34:26

When kids play "king of the hill," the one at the top
of the hill has a distinct natural advantage over the others because all the "king" has to do is push over the others climbing up the hill, and gravity is on the side of the
king.

Jesus is the King of kings and the Lord of lords. And,
of course, He has all the advantages; He's God!

Why does God care about a hill? It can only be ex-
plained by understanding that the reference is to Jerusalem, which is situated on a very high hill (Mount
Zion). It had been the scene of many of the most significant events in the Bible. Jesus wept over it because its
people did not realize that their Savior had come and
they would kill Him. Maybe we are more like Jerusalem
than we care to admit. We have seen God's blessing in
our lives, time and time again, yet we ignore Him and
disobey Him daily. He has more than enough reasons
to weep over us, too.

Kings are also supposed to be merciful. Let's try to be
noble and merciful with everyone we encounter today.

Reservations Required

Then he asked, "Haven't you reserved any *blessing* for me?"

Genesis 27:36

The story of Esau and Jacob is the story of life. Both of the brothers had what the other one wanted. Jacob, the younger of the twin brothers, had food that Esau wanted, and Esau had a birthright that Jacob wanted. The deal was done, and each got what they wanted. Later, though, Jacob goes for the jugular. He steals the only spiritual asset Esau owned, the blessing each father bestowed on his chosen successor. Esau is left begging with tears for any other blessing his father, Isaac, may have left. He did have one more blessing of sorts, and he tells Esau he will always serve Jacob and live in an arid land.

This is a story of life because everyone wants what they can't have, and some people, like Jacob, will do what it takes to get it. Why did God bless him for his underhandedness? Jacob knew that the blessing was from God, not just his earthly father Isaac; he wanted it because he wanted to be closer to God. Although it may seem strange, God did, in fact, bless his actions because his motives were pure, while Esau most likely only saw the blessing as a measure of his prestige and power.

God has many blessings reserved for those of us whose motives toward Him and others are pure. What He despises are those who are only motivated by prestige, power, position, and money.

We all do a good job of hiding our motives.

What's going to motivate us today?

The Great One

I will make your name great, and you will be
a *blessing*.

Genesis 12:2

What does it mean to be great? Many people would
say being rich makes you great, but money doesn't solve
heartbreaks and heartaches. Others would say fame
makes you great, but it seems like the famous people
are always going in or out of rehab for one addiction or
another. Some might say that being healthy makes you
great, but we'll all surely die, so health only postpones
the inevitable.

Here, God is speaking to Abraham. He is promising
to make his name great because Abraham believed in
God, believed in God's promises, and lived his life in
obedience to God's instructions. It was his faith, and
his faith lived out by his actions, that made him great.

Based on that standard, how can we achieve greatness today?

Lip Service

You will be [...] *blessed* in the country.

Deuteronomy 28:3

We associate things from the "country" in several ways. Sometimes the country sounds peaceful, simple, and wholesome, like picturing a pleasant farm scene. At other times, country can seem a bit backward and slow. People from cities sometimes look down on people from rural areas. For years, country music was not afforded the respect it now has because it was seen as the music of rednecks and cowboys.

Thankfully, God doesn't play favorites, and He doesn't care where we live. He only cares *how* we live. What He especially wants to eliminate in us is prideful arrogance. The truth is, we often think we are better than others. It may not be as clear as city vs. country; often, it can be as simple as not letting another driver in front of us in traffic because we don't want to.

God's desire for us to be humble, not prideful, is one of the most fundamental traits that He wants to develop in us. We can take the easy path, acknowledge our faults and pray for His help, or we can ignore His urgings and suffer the consequences of His frustration with us.

He doesn't want lip service, He wants action. How are you going to act today?

DECEMBER 27

If You Please

He will *bless* the fruit of your womb, the crops
of your land—your grain, new wine and olive
oil—the calves of your herds and the lambs of
your flocks in the land He swore to your ancestors to give you.

Deuteronomy 7:13

Many of us are always worried about how much we
eat. Diets and exercise are tools to help beat the battle of
the bulge. We never have to worry about having *enough*
to eat, though; our society creates so much food that
we throw tons of it away every year. In biblical times,
famine and drought could easily lead to starvation and
death for whole families.

Here, God is telling Israel that if they follow His
ways, they will always have an abundance of food. "If"
is a very small word with large consequences. If we
walk closer to God, we can change our lives by learning
from Him and being submissive to Him. If instead, we
decide to please ourselves and follow our own instincts
and hunches, we may miss out on the blessings that
could otherwise be ours.

Which "if" will you choose today?

Setting the Standard

I will *bless* her so that she will be a mother of
nations; kings of peoples will come from her.

Genesis 17:16

We all have a mother, and a good mom can make
us or break us. She can make us by being strict but
supportive, kind and cuddly, and always committed
to the best for her children. Sometimes when we were
younger, what our mother decided was best made us
mad; in turn, we would be disrespectful and difficult
to live with. She acted out of love, but we acted out of
selfishness.

Here, the woman God is blessing is Sarah, the wife
of Abraham, who was about to become the mother of
Isaac at the age of 90 years old. Imagine the emotional and physical strength it took to do that! She did it,
though, and through her faith in God, Isaac grew up
into the man from whom all Jews would come, including Jesus. She set the standard and set it high.

What standard will we choose today: high, low, or
mediocre?

Seems Like Forever

...for You, O Lord, have blessed it, and it will be *blessed* forever.

1 Chronicles 17:27

Forever is a concept that can go one of two ways. If the "forever" is something good, like "I'll love you forever," then it sounds amazing. But if the forever is something bad, like "you'll rot in hell forever," then it sounds awful.

Here, David is thanking God for the blessing he had just received. God promised David that one of his descendants would always serve as king of Israel, forever! All they had to do was obey God's commands and laws, which they failed to do. Ultimately, Jesus fulfilled this promise, though, because He is a descendant of David and will rule God's kingdom forever.

Rather than focus on forever, we should focus on today. What can we do today that will make our forever better?

Two Sides of the Same Coin

Bless and do not curse.

Romans 12:14

There is nothing more opposite than a *blessing* and a curse. Blessings are meant to bestow good things on the recipient, while curses are meant to inflict pain and misery.

It's almost always easier to curse than to bless. We curse at other drivers, coworkers, family members, and anyone who frustrates us. Blessing others is rare because, unless it is someone we are extremely close to, we usually don't appreciate people enough to encourage or refresh them.

Jesus came to bless us by offering eternal life to everyone who believes that He is the Son of God. Simple enough. He also said that those who ignore His call will face the curse of eternal damnation. Again, simple enough.

It's like we have one coin, and we get to choose one side or the other. If we died today, which side of the coin would win?

End of the Road

Even though he sought the *blessing* with tears,
he could not change what he had done.

Hebrews 12:17

As the year draws to a close, it is important to revisit Esau. As we know, he was Jacob's twin brother who sold his birthright for a bowl of stew. Later, Jacob tricked their father Isaac into giving him, not Esau, Isaac's *blessing*.

Unfortunately, we are more like Esau than Jesus most of the time. We "sell" our Christian values for things our culture offers all the time. Whether it is bending our opinions so as not to stand out or living our lives in such a way that no one would identify us as Christian, we constantly compromise.

Unlike Esau—thank God—we have a Savior, Jesus, Who forgives our sins and shortcomings and *blesses* us despite our continued screw-ups and denials. He wipes our tears and comforts us.

As we approach the end of the year, and for some, the end of the road, what can we do today and every day to act more like Jesus and less like Esau?

Endnotes

1 Luke 6:38

2 Micah 6:8

3 Luke 12:48

4 Stewart Michael (book), Brecher Irving (screenplay), *Bye Bye Birdie* (1963)

5 Matthew 5:45

6 Job 12:5

7 1 Peter 5:7

8 James 2:18

9 Proverbs 9:10

10 John 7:37-39

11 Luke 6:32

12 Proverbs 4:7

13 James 1:5

14 Matthew 6:33

15 Malachi 3:10

16 Hebrews 4:16

17 Zechariah 2:8

18 Deuteronomy 31:6

19 Matthew 23:37

20 Song of Solomon 8:6

21 1 Corinthians 7:5

22 Matthew 13:45-46

23 John 14:6

24 1 Corinthians 7:5

25 Micah 6:8

26 Acts 4:32

27 Hebrews 12:1-2

28 Romans 12:20

29 Matthew 6:25-34

30 Galatians 3:29

31 2 Corinthians 5:21

32 1 Chronicles 13:14

33 Romans 1:29

34 Galatians 3:13

35 2 Corinthians 9:7

36 Luke 10:25-37

37 Matthew 15:14

38 Proverbs 18:11

39 Psalm 34:8

40 1 Timothy 6:10

41 Chamlee, Virginia. "Americans Now Spend More at Restaurants Than Grocery Stores." Eater.com. https://www.eater.com/2016/6/16/11954062/restaurant-spending-outpaces-grocery-stores (retrieved 11/4/2018)

42 Philippians 4:7

43 2 Samuel 7:18

44 Matthew 6:15

45 Proverbs 17:28 ESV

46 Matthew 5:5

CPSIA information can be obtained
at www.ICGtesting.com
Printed in the USA
BVHW031657061222
653569BV00014B/892

9 781637 690901